Catalyst
by Tutorials

Marin Benčević, Nick Bonatsakis & Andy Pereira

Catalyst by Tutorials

By Marin Benčević, Nick Bonatsakis & Andy Pereira

Copyright ©2020 Razeware LLC.

ISBN: 978-1-950325-31-3

About the Authors

Marin Benčević is an author of this book. He is an image processing researcher as well as an iOS developer who likes to work on cool iOS apps and games, nerd out about programming, and he can talk for far too long with you about coffee. He also has a chubby cat.

Andy Pereira is an author of this book. He is an iOS developer in Atlanta, GA. He enjoys traveling the world with his wife, learning new cultures, and playing guitar.

Nick Bonatsakis is an author of this book. He is an accomplished software engineer with over a decade of experience in mobile development across both Android and iOS. He is a passionate technologist, musician, father and husband. He currently works as an independent consultant under his own company, Velocity Raptor Inc.

About the Editors

Ehab Amer is a tech editor for this book. He is a very enthusiastic Lead iOS developer with a very diverse experience. From building games to enterprise applications and POCs, especially when exploring new technologies. In his spare time, TV shows take the majority, followed by video games. When away from the screen, he goes with his friends for escape room experiences or to explore the underwater world through diving.

Pinal Naik is a tech editor of this book. She is passionate about iOS and AI technologies and creator of the iOS app xplooor. When not coding, you'll find her immersed in a book, traveling or spending time with her two super-energetic boys. She hopes to inspire a lot more women to become developers and app creators.

Jerry Beers is the final pass editor of this book. He is co-founder of Five Pack Creative, a mobile development company specializing in iOS development. He is passionate about creating well-crafted code and teaching others. You can find his company's site at fivepackcreative.com.

Brian Schick is a tech editor for this book. He lives in Portland, Oregon, and is Mobile Team Lead with Beezwax Datatools. He's mastered technologies ranging from deep data back-end tools to front-end UI and UX best practices, and is currently happily obsessed with all things Swift. When not coding, Brian can be found hiking, tending bamboo, woodworking, or hanging out with the world's two bestest dogs and a good craft brew or three.

About the Artist

Vicki Wenderlich is the designer and artist of the cover of this book. She is Ray's wife and business partner. She is a digital artist who creates illustrations, game art and a lot of other art or design work for the tutorials and books on raywenderlich.com. When she's not making art, she loves hiking, a good glass of wine and attempting to create the perfect cheese plate.

Dedications

"To my mom, for always pushing me to do things I'm too lazy to do."

— Marin Benčević

"To my parents, for providing the education and support that ultimately made it possible for me to write this book."

— Nick Bonatsakis

"To my wife, Angela, for believing in me, and encouraging all I do. I wouldn't be where I am without you."

— Andy Pereira

Table of Contents

Book License

By purchasing *Catalyst by Tutorials*, you have the following license:

- You are allowed to use and/or modify the source code in *Catalyst by Tutorials* in as many apps as you want, with no attribution required.

- You are allowed to use and/or modify all art, images and designs that are included in *Catalyst by Tutorials* in as many apps as you want, but must include this attribution line somewhere inside your app: "Artwork/images/designs: from *Catalyst by Tutorials*, available at www.raywenderlich.com".

- The source code included in *Catalyst by Tutorials* is for your personal use only. You are NOT allowed to distribute or sell the source code in *Catalyst by Tutorials* without prior authorization.

- This book is for your personal use only. You are NOT allowed to sell this book without prior authorization, or distribute it to friends, coworkers or students; they would need to purchase their own copies.

All materials provided with this book are provided on an "as is" basis, without warranty of any kind, express or implied, including but not limited to the warranties of merchantability, fitness for a particular purpose and noninfringement. In no event shall the authors or copyright holders be liable for any claim, damages or other liability, whether in an action or contract, tort or otherwise, arising from, out of or in connection with the software or the use or other dealings in the software.

All trademarks and registered trademarks appearing in this guide are the properties of their respective owners.

Before You Begin

This section tells you a few things you need to know before you get started, such as what you'll need for hardware and software, where to find the project files for this book, and more.

What You Need

To follow along with the tutorials in this book, you'll need the following:

- A Mac running macOS Big Sur (11.0) or later.

- Xcode 12.2 or later.

- An Apple Developer account. You can enroll at https://developer.apple.com/programs/. For development, the free account will suffice, but if you want to distribute the apps you build, you'll need a paid account.

You can use the simulator that comes with Xcode for all of the chapters.

> **Note**: At the time this is published, macOS Big Sur is still in beta. If necessary, content will be updated as updates come out. Until Big Sur is released, apps built for it will not be uploadable to the App Store.

Book Source Code & Forums

Book source code

The materials for this book are all available in the GitHub repository here:

- https://github.com/raywenderlich/cat-materials/tree/editions/2.0

You can download the entire set of materials for the book from that page.

Forum

We've also set up an official forum for the book at https://forums.raywenderlich.com/c/books/catalyst-by-tutorials. This is a great place to ask questions about the book or to submit any errors you may find.

About the Cover

Catalyst by Tutorials Cover

The hermit crab is a fascinating, adaptable creature; of the approximately 1,100 species of hermit crab, most of them spend their lives living inside the discarded shells of other marine creatures. When shells are scarce, hermit crabs call upon their resourcefulness to find a suitable home for themselves; they have been known to inhabit objects such as hollow pieces of wood, stone, or even discarded cans when a suitable shell can't be found.

As further proof of the hermit crab's flexibility and adaptability, some species even give up the nomadic crab lifestyle and live inside fixed structures left behind by animals such as corals or sponges, while a few species head for a better life on land.

Catalyst apps are happy in multiple environments as well; when well-built, they can easily adapt to the iPadOS ecosystem as well as the macOS ecosystem in a nearly seamless manner. If your iPad app is useful enough that it makes sense to bridge it to a desktop operating system, Catalyst will be there to help your iPad app *scuttle* over to its new home on macOS. I just wonder what a hermit crab would think about all of the *shell* commands on macOS?

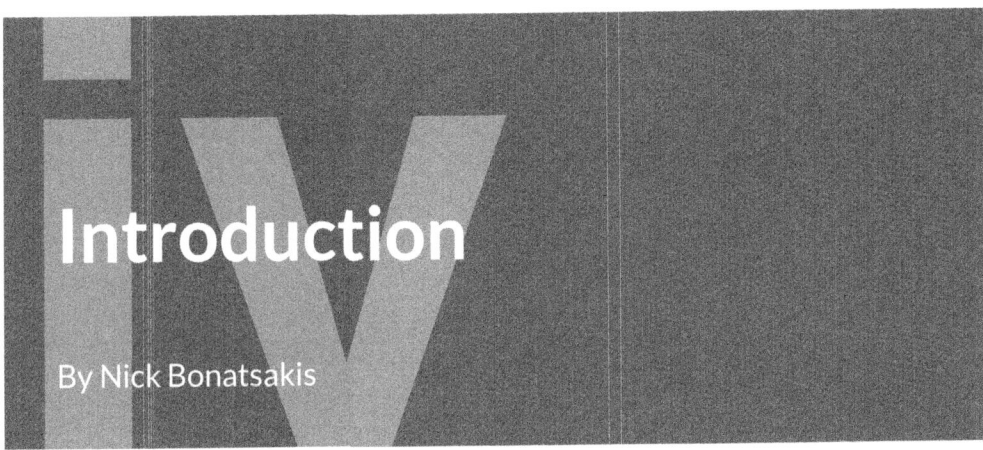

Introduction

By Nick Bonatsakis

Since the introduction of the first iPhone, Apple has been building and maintaining two parallel operating systems: macOS and iOS. Both are based on Darwin but optimized for different types of interaction. As time passed, the apps and features on macOS and iOS started to converge slowly. It became very common for developers to create and support apps that ran on multiple types of Apple devices, from iPhone, iPad and Mac.

The trouble with building an app that runs on both iOS and Mac is that you need to learn and use two different UI frameworks: UIKit and AppKit. And, therefore need to maintain two distinct codebases. While it is, of course, possible to share some code using frameworks, the entirety of an app's UI-related code effectively needs to be done twice.

With the arrival of Catalyst, it is now possible to bring an iPad app to the Mac using a single, UIKit-based codebase. With minimal effort, your iPad app can function quite well on macOS, and with a bit of additional effort, can become a world-class Mac citizen.

What is this book?

Throughout this book, you'll work with a single sample project called *Journalyst*. Starting with a basic iPhone-only app, you'll learn how to first enhance for iPad with some of the features that apply to both iPad and Mac. Once your iPad app really shines, you'll take the next step by optimizing it to run on Mac using Catalyst. Finally, you'll learn how to build and distribute your new Mac app to both the Mac App Store and independently.

Who is this book written for?

This book is for you if:

• You have an existing iPhone app that you want to bring to iPad or Mac.

• You have an existing iPad app that you want to bring to Mac.

• You're just starting out building a new app, and you want to build for iPhone, iPad and Mac.

How to use this book

This book is organized into three sections, carrying you through optimizing an iPhone app for iPad, then bringing that iPad app to Mac, and finally distributing the Mac app. It is best read linearly, but if you already have a great iPad app, you can jump straight to the Mac section. Do note, however, that Apple has added some new iPad capabilities alongside the introduction of Catalyst that you may not be familiar with. Even if you have an existing iPad app, it would be a good idea to review the first section before proceeding.

Catalyst

If you've made it this far, you likely know what Catalyst is. But in case you need a refresher, it is Apple's mechanism for bringing iPad apps to the Mac. Introduced in macOS 10.15, it enables you to simply tick a checkbox in your UIKit-based Xcode project and begin running your app on the Mac.

Starting in macOS 10.15, many of Apple's own apps that run across iOS and macOS have been built using Catalyst, including Maps, News, Voice Memos, Podcasts, and Reminders. If you've used any of these apps on Mac and iPad, you'll note that they are similar in structure, but the apps feel quite genuine on their respective platforms. Even when you run your iPad app on Mac without modification, you'll find that it already adopts many of the Mac-standard UI idioms, it's not just your iPad app running on a desktop simulator.

Here's a look at how the Reminders app looks, first running on iPad:

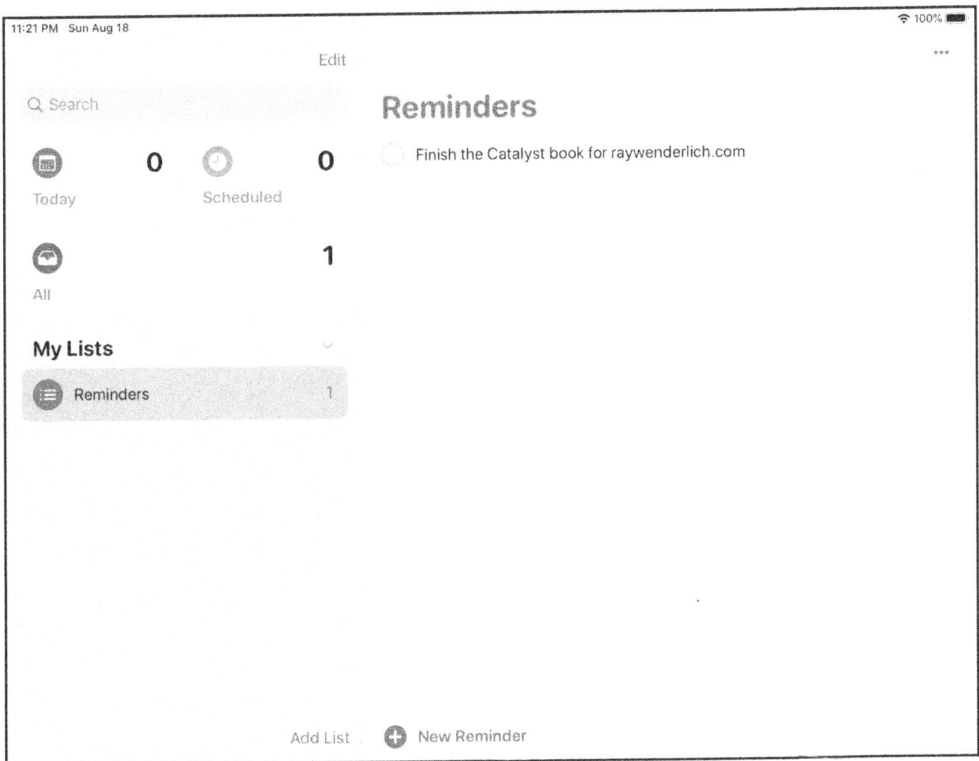

And now, on Mac:

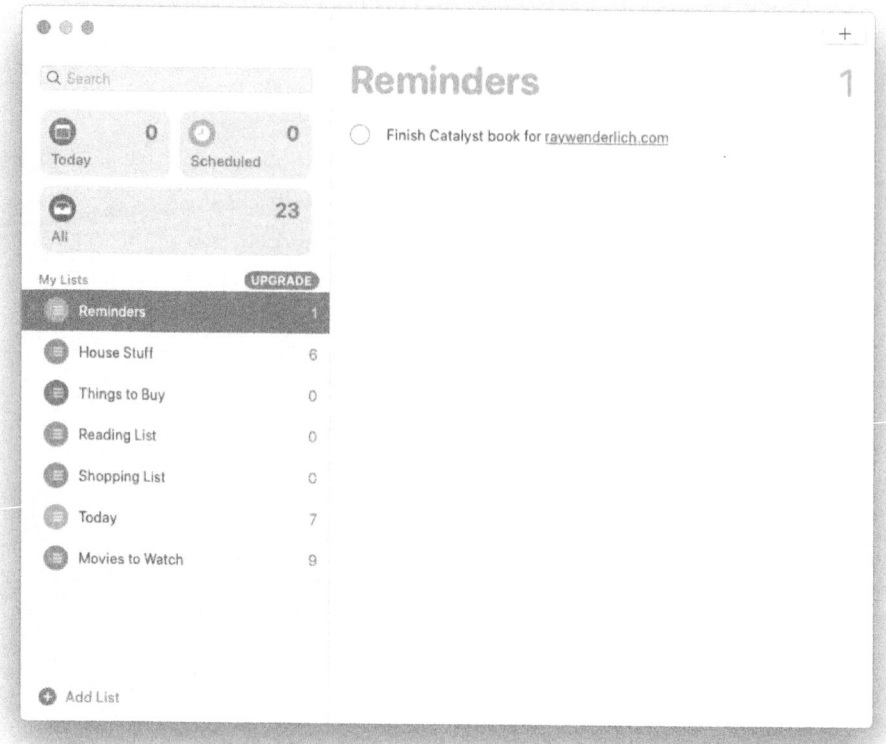

A few more things to note about Catalyst before you learn more about how it works:

First, you've probably noticed the word "iPad" used over "iOS" or "iPhone and iPad" when Catalyst is being discussed. This is not a coincidence. Catalyst is only available for apps that support iPad. This is because iPad apps have already gone through changes required to take advantage of things like a larger display, keyboard, multi-window, etc. Thus, they make a much smoother transition to the Mac.

Secondly, while Catalyst apps run on Mac, they are not AppKit apps, and can not easily accomplish some of the feats achieved by AppKit apps. Catalyst is a powerful first step towards a new way of building Mac apps, but a first step nonetheless. For this reason, AppKit is still a fully supported method for building Mac-only apps and is going to be the best approach for some classes of apps.

Lastly, when you build using Catalyst, you'll end up with a separate Mac binary, although you're using one single codebase. This is unlike universal app binaries for iOS that run on both iPhone and iPad. It also means that your app has to be distributed separately, just like any Mac app, on the Mac App Store or independently.

Now, let's take a deeper dive into how Catalyst does what it does.

Catalyst under the hood

As mentioned earlier, Catalyst is not merely taking your iOS app and running it in a simulated Mac environment. Nor is it some variation of AppKit, which still exists separate from Catalyst and UIKit. So what is it then?

Well, it is UIKit running under the x86 architecture, and rendering Mac-style UI. But, it's not just UIKit. It's also many of the system frameworks you know and love, some that were already available on Mac, and some that were not. Because AppKit remains as a first-class method for creating Mac apps, Apple now has two stacks for doing so.

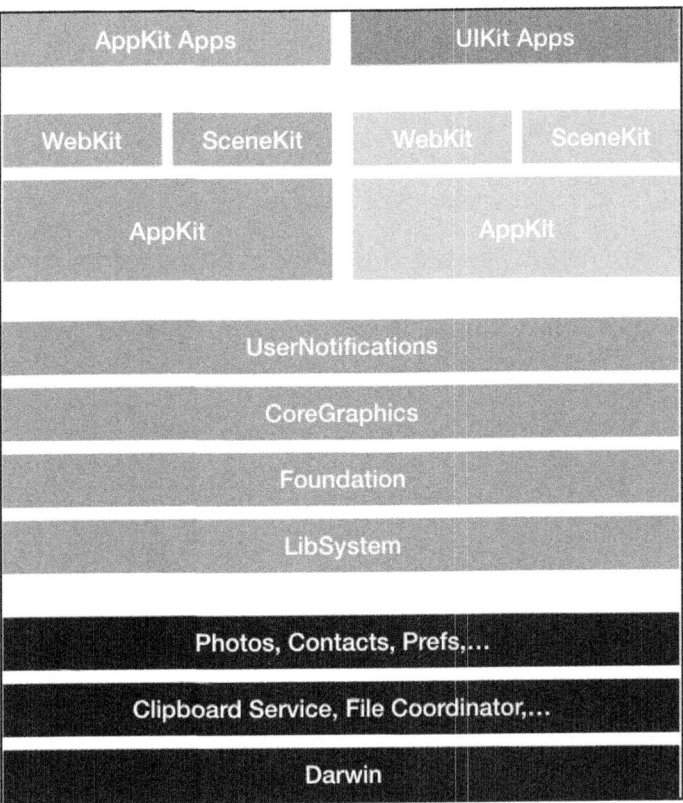

Instead of maintaining two entirely separate framework stacks, Apple has wisely unified frameworks where possible and left them separate otherwise. In the above diagram, you can see where the stacks continue to have separate components (WebKit, SceneKit, etc.), and where they converge (frameworks like Foundation and various types of user data stores).

Framework availability

While Apple has made the experience of running iPad apps on Mac quite frictionless, not all frameworks available on iOS are available on macOS. Frameworks that take advantage of hardware features found only on mobile devices are not available on macOS. Therefore, code that uses these frameworks must compile out when building under Catalyst.

You'll learn more about how to conditionally include or exclude code when running under UIKit for Mac later on in the book.

UI availability

Much like with frameworks, there isn't always going to be a 1:1 analog between an iOS UI component and a Mac equivalent. As you start porting your iPad apps to Mac, you'll notice that many controls on iOS, such as `UITabBar`, don't exist on Mac. So, they must be replaced with suitable Mac-style alternatives.

Tabs, for example, are typically found in macOS toolbars at the top of windows as opposed to a dedicated lower area on iOS. The top of a window is where a user expects to find hierarchical controls on a desktop app. Whereas, for one-handed touch device use, it is more ergonomic to have tabs at the bottom. In this case, you could simply render a standard `UITabBar` when running on iOS, but move those same tabs to `NSToolbar` for the app window when on macOS.

Which apps should make use of Catalyst?

Now that you have a good idea of how Catalyst works, it's worth asking the question: Which apps make sense to be ported to the Mac? The answer, as you'd expect, is: Not all of them.

In general, any iPad app can be configured to run on Mac. But, if your app falls into one of the below buckets, it might be particularly ripe for Catalytic conversion:

- **Apps with comprehensive iPad support.** If your app is already well supported on iPad, and you've put off making a Mac app for lack of time or wanting to maintain another codebase, now might be the time to bring it to Mac.

- **Apps with old or poorly maintained AppKit counterparts.** Likewise, if you already have a Mac version of your iOS app, but it has fallen into disrepair or is out of date, it may be a good idea to sunset it in favor of a Catalyst app based on your iPad project.

Conversely, if any of the bullets in the below list describe your app, you may not need to use Catalyst:

- **Apps that make extensive use of mobile-device hardware.** An app that is entirely based on ARKit for example (like an AR-based game), would be almost entirely non-functional on Mac.

- **Apps that leverage cross-platform engines.** A game build using a tool like Unity, for example, can already be built for Mac without the use of Catalyst.

- **Apps that already have well-supported AppKit versions.** Many iOS apps already have very well done and maintained AppKit counterparts. In these cases, there isn't a huge benefit to switching to using Catalyst.

Where to go from here?

Now that you've been introduced to Catalyst and have a general understanding of what it does and how it works, it's time to put it to the test. In the first chapter, you're going to tick some checkboxes and find out how easy it is to get started running your app on both iPad and Mac.

Section I: Making a Great iPad App

Catalyst is all about letting you use code you've written for iOS on macOS. But not just any code. At least for now, you can only run code that is written for iPad on a Mac. And because most of the code will run on both platforms, before you dive in to running your app on your Mac, there are a few things you should do to make your code ready.

In this section, you'll take an app written to run on iPhone and adapt it to run on iPad. Then you'll add some features to make it behave like a first-class iPad citizen. And through the magic of Catalyst, these features will make your Mac app better too!

Chapter 1: The Checkbox

By Nick Bonatsakis

In the introduction, you learned about what Catalyst is, how it works and the initial considerations you'll make when using it to bring your app to the Mac.

In this chapter, you're going to get your first look at the sample app that you'll be interacting with for the remainder of this book. Once you familiarize yourself with the basic functionality and architecture, you'll take your first steps toward bringing the app to macOS.

By the end of this chapter, you'll have learned:

- The basic functionality and architecture of the sample app.
- The Xcode project changes needed to get your iOS app running on macOS.
- Which features Catalyst gives you for free when running on the Mac.
- Which features don't work as well out-of-the-box.

It's time to get comfortable with the sample app that'll be your companion for the remainder of your Catalytic journey.

The sample app: Journalyst

Meet the last journaling app you'll ever need; it's called **Journalyst** and it has been designed from the ground-up to be the best way to chronicle your daily adventures. Start by taking it for a quick test drive.

Open **Journalyst.xcodeproj** from the starter project for this chapter in Xcode and then build and run.

You should see the main journal entry list screen:

Here you can see all the journal entries you've created as well as an add button in the upper right that will add a new entry when tapped. Try tapping the add button a few times to see new entries get added to the list. Next, tap on any entry in the list to dive into the journal entry detail screen.

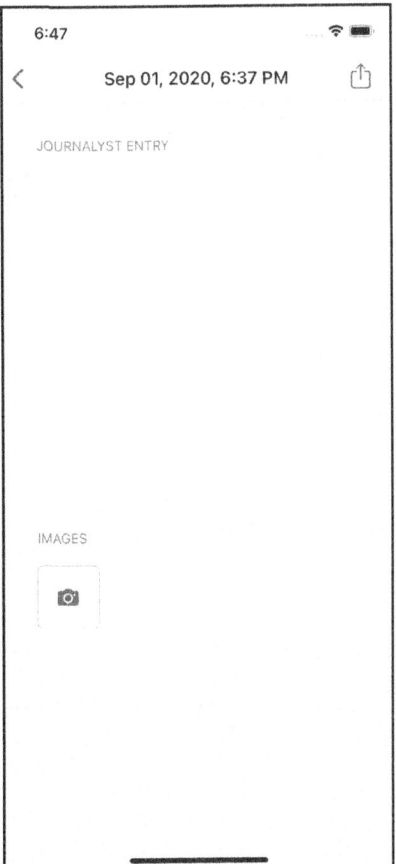

At the top of this screen, there is a text area where you can add the textual content for this entry. Below the text area, you'll find a button that you can tap to add images. Finally, there is a **Share** button in the upper-right that, when tapped, will bring up the standard iOS activity view, allowing you to share the content. Spend a few moments tapping on the various controls, and then get ready to move on to the code.

In the Xcode project, expand the **Journalyst** group in the navigation pane. Once you do so, you'll see a handful of groups that house the various architectural components that make up the app, alongside the standard files you'd expect in a new Xcode project.

Here's a brief breakdown of the files:

Models

- **Entry**: A class that represents a single journal entry in the app.

- **EntryDataSource**: A datasource class that works with table view to update its data.

View Controllers

- **MainTableViewController**: A table view controller that renders the journal entries list, which is the main screen of the app.

- **EntryTableViewController**: A table view controller that renders the detail screen for a single journal entry.

Views

- **EntryTableViewCell**: A table view cell that represents a single journal entry on the main screen.

- **ImageCollectionViewCell**: A collection view cell that renders an image attachment in the image area of the single journal entry screen.

Take some time to dig into each of the above files so you can get a feel for the overall structure and data flow. The app is not overly complex, but it will serve as a great starting point for taking you through all the aspects of Catalyst.

Once you feel comfortable with the project, it's time to take your first steps towards Mac-ifying your first app.

The iPad checkbox

"Wait, what? I thought we were migrating this app to run on the Mac. What's this iPad business about?" You may have noticed that the Journalyst app is currently configured and designed to run on iPhone only. Well, it turns out that an iPhone app, even a great one, doesn't translate well to the much larger screen of a Mac.

iPhone apps are optimized for single-window use, where you see one screen at a time on a very confined display size. They aren't typically concerned with things like drag-and-drop, multi-tasking, split views, keyboard shortcuts and all manner of other functionality commonly found in Mac apps.

iPad apps, on the other hand, are concerned with the above features, run on comparable display sizes, and thus have far more in common with Mac apps. For this reason, Apple wisely decided that, for an iOS app to run on macOS, it must be capable of running on iPad. So if you were hoping to take your iPhone-only app straight to macOS, you're in for a bit more work than you may have expected. This book will guide you through the process of both bringing your iPhone app to iPad, and then bringing that iPad app to the Mac.

Apple states that the first step in making a great Mac app using Catalyst is making a great iPad app. The more your app is designed to be a good citizen on the iPad, the easier it will be to bring it to macOS using Catalyst. So before you can check the "Mac" checkbox, you'll have to check the "iPad" checkbox.

In the Xcode project, click on the top-level **Journalyst** entry in the navigation pane, select the main app target, and click on the **General** tab. You should see three checkboxes within the **Deployment Info** section, only "iPhone" is currently activated.

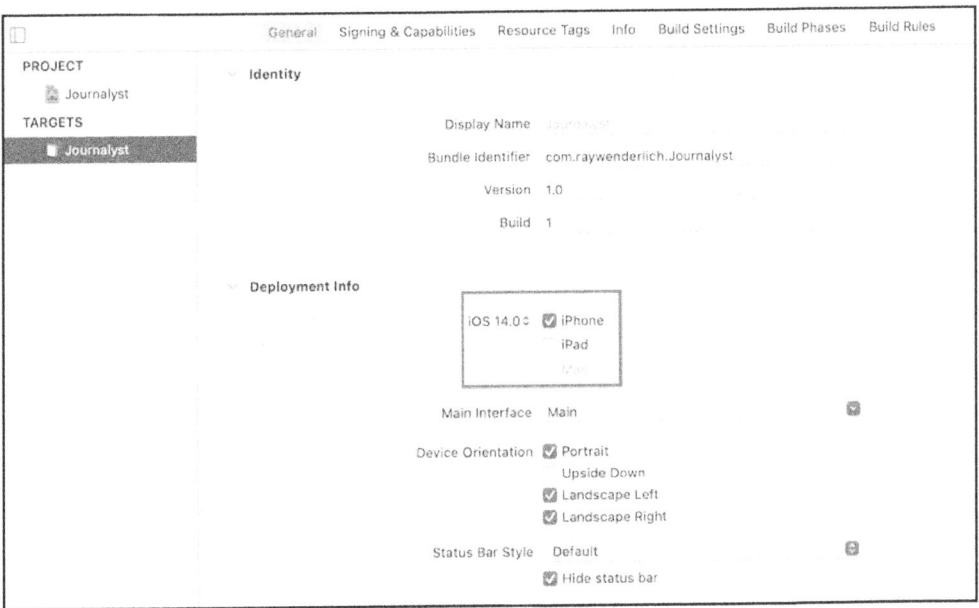

Check the **iPad** checkbox. Just like that, you've added support for iPad. Select an iPad simulator as the run target then build and run to have a look at the fruits of your labors.

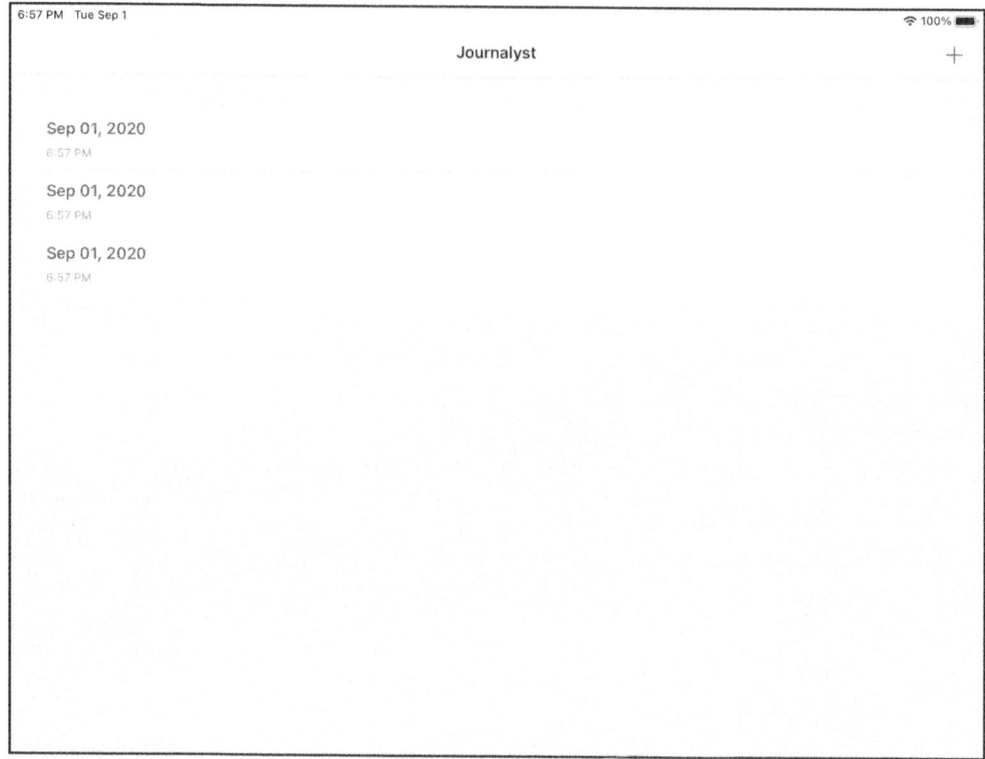

And there it is! The Journalyst app running on the iPad... Looks great right? Well, maybe not so much.

Through the magic of auto-layout, nothing looks broken per se, and app features still work. However, what you see is an inflated version of the iPhone app. It doesn't look or feel like a first-class iPad citizen. You can do much better than this, and in the chapters that follow, you will.

Be aware that some features are downright broken when running on iPad. If you try to activate anything that would bring up an action sheet, such as adding an image or sharing an entry, the app will crash. You'll learn why this is the case, and how to fix it in the next chapter.

But this chapter is all about instant gratification via checkboxes, so put your dreams of creating the next hit iPad app to the side for now and prepare to see the app running on the Mac.

The Mac checkbox

And now the checkbox you've been waiting for! Back in the **General** tab of the **Journalist** target settings, go ahead and check the "Mac" checkbox.

Note: Since Catalyst is only supported on macOS 10.15 or higher, if you are on an older version of macOS, this checkbox will be disabled. Make sure you are using macOS 10.15 or higher and Xcode 11 or higher before proceeding.

You'll notice that, this time, unlike when you checked the "iPad" checkbox, Xcode prompts you to make some changes to the project. Allow it to do so, and the following changes will be made:

- An entitlement for App Sandbox is added to the **Journalyst.entitlements** file. Apps that are distributed on the Mac App Store must incorporate sandboxing, which you'll learn more about in a later chapter that covers distributing your Catalyst app.

- A new run destination for **My Mac** is added to the project so that you can run the app from Xcode.

- Incompatible frameworks, app extensions and other embedded content are excluded from the Mac build. In this case, there aren't any yet.

Once you've enabled the Mac checkbox and accepted project changes, you'll notice a new dropdown to the right of "Mac". Go ahead and click it, then select "Optimize Interface for Mac".

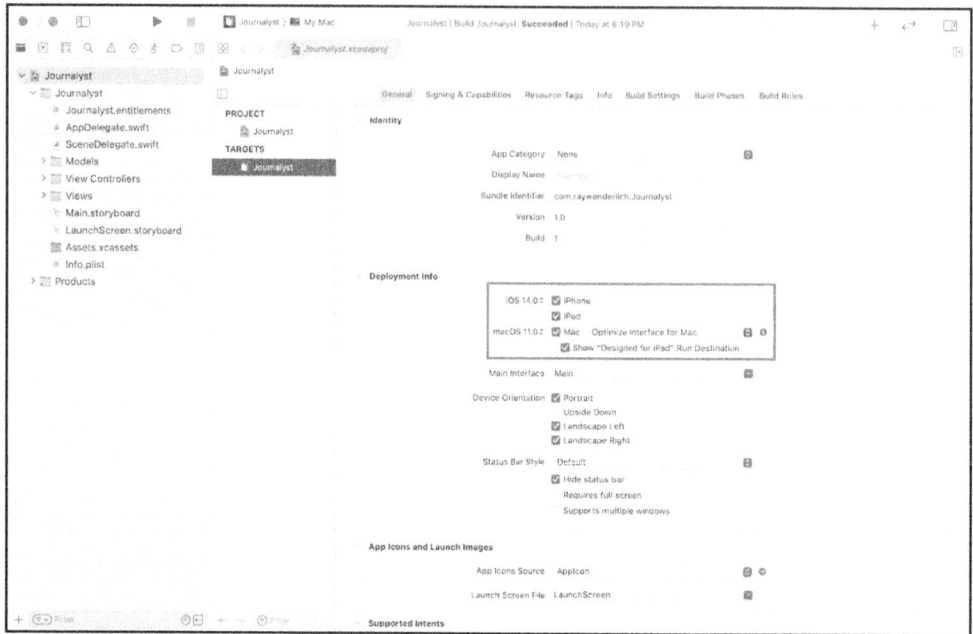

From Apple's Xcode release notes on the option:

> When bringing iPad apps to macOS, you can now use the Optimize Interface for Mac target setting to use native macOS controls and Mac resolution

Since your ultimate goal is to make an app that looks and feels like a first-class macOS app when running on the Mac, you want the interface to be optimized accordingly.

Go to the **Signing & Capabilities** tab of the **Journalyst** target settings and under **Signing**, you'll notice you have bundle ids for iOS and macOS platforms. Under macOS platform, you'll notice **Use iOS Bundle Identifier** is checked.

Go ahead and uncheck the **Use iOS Bundle Identifier** checkbox. Then, create a macOS Bundle identifier as *maccatalyst.com.raywenderlich.Journalyst*.

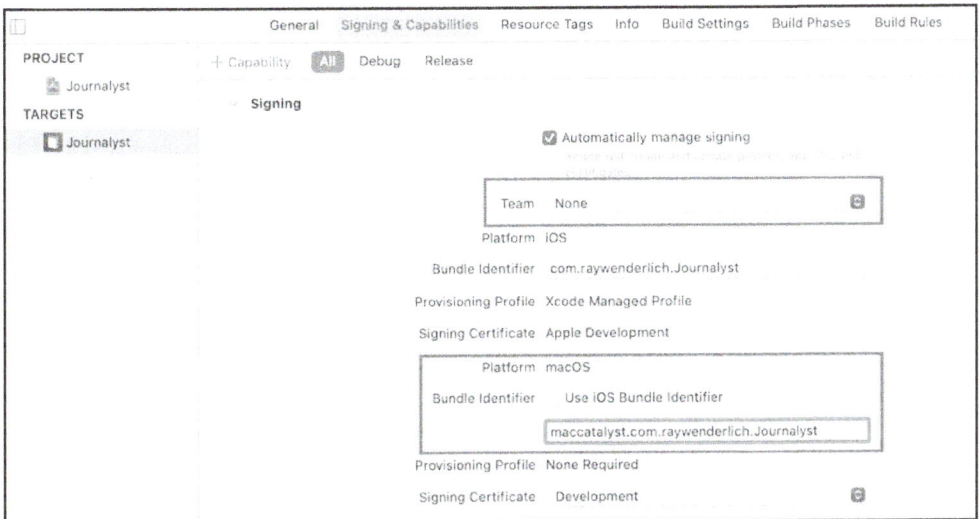

The last thing you'll need to do before running the Mac app is to specify code signing information. This step isn't necessary when running the iOS app on simulators, but in this case, your Mac is a real device, so the bundle needs to be signed.

Go ahead and select a team. Make sure **Automatically Manage Signing** is enabled, and Xcode will take care of the rest.

Finally, change the run destination to **My Mac**, build and run, then bask in the glory that is your first Catalyst app!

Much like when you ran the app on iPad for the first time, the basic functionality is there after applying almost zero effort, but the app in its current form leaves much to be desired. Still, Catalyst gives you a whole lot of Mac goodness for free, so poke around, and you'll find that your Mac app already has the following features:

- A basic Mac menu bar.

- Support for trackpad, mouse and keyboard input.

- Support for window resizing and full-screen display.

- Mac-style scroll bars.

- Copy-and-paste support.

- Basic drag-and-drop support.

- Support for system Touch Bar controls.

But it's not all rainbows and checkboxes at this point — there's still a lot of work you'll need to do to make this app a first-class Mac experience. Some of the more notable features that are currently missing are:

- Multi-window support.

- A better navigation structure, given the larger screen size (a split view would do nicely here).

- Extended drag-and-drop support for things like dragging images into journal entries.

- Extended keyboard support for things like shortcuts.

- Extended mouse support for custom contextual menus.

- A Mac-style preferences window for app settings.

- A better look and feel for the app that aligns it more with what you commonly see on macOS.

- Better support for the menu bar, toolbar and the touch bar that go beyond what you get out-of-the-box.

That list might look daunting, but the remainder of this book will guide you through the process of implementing all of these features and more. The rest of the chapters in Section 1 will cover the features that you'll add to turn Journalyst into a great iPad app. Section 2 will then cover the process of turning your great iPad app into an even greater Mac app. Rounding things out, Section 3 will walk you through the finer points of packaging and distributing your new Mac app.

Key points

- Journalyst is a basic journaling app that you'll be improving throughout this book.

- Before you can make a great Mac app using Catalyst, you need to make a great iPad app.

- Catalyst gives you plenty of Mac functionality for free.

- To make a truly great Mac app using Catalyst, you need to go above and beyond what comes out-of-the-box, covered above.

Where to go from here?

In this chapter, you became familiar with Journalyst, the sample app you'll update throughout the rest of this book as you learn how to bring apps from iPhone to iPad, and then to the Mac. You took the first steps along this path by configuring the app to run on both iPad and Mac by changing the Xcode project configuration. Finally, you learned about which features Catalyst provides out of the box and which ones require additional effort to enable.

Chapter 2: Migrating to Split View Controller

By Andy Pereira

The split view controller provides a way to manage two view controllers at the same time. The split view controller takes advantage of the iPad's significantly larger screen size, making it easy to display a master-detail style interface. This also makes it easy to adapt to the screen size of the device someone may be using. In this chapter, you'll convert the iPhone "master-detail" pattern found in Journalyst to a split view controller, then update the UI to take advantage of the view.

Getting started

Open the starter project for the chapter. Select an iPad Pro simulator in the active scheme, then build and run the app. In its current state, the iPad version of Journalyst requires you to select an entry before you can see the details.

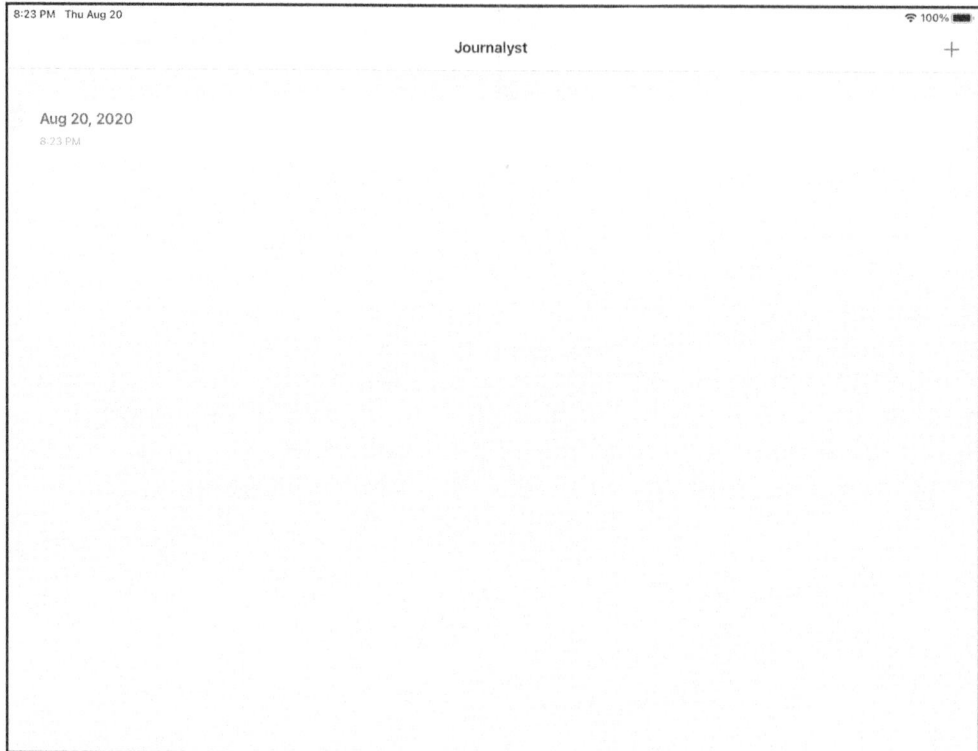

Integrating Split View Controller

Open **Main.storyboard** and select the **Entry Table View Controller** scene. From the menu bar, select **Editor ▸ Embed In ▸ Navigation Controller**.

This inserts a navigation controller and keeps the segue you had before, but you need to change a property of it. Select the segue between the Journalyst scene and your new navigation controller and in the **Attributes inspector** change the **Kind** to "Show Detail".

The segue already has a segue action attached to it (from the starter project), and you won't need to change that.

Now, open **MainTableViewController.swift** and add the following property:

```
// MARK: - Properties
var entryTableViewController: EntryTableViewController?
```

The segue action connection didn't need to change, but with your new navigation controller, the code it runs will. Replace `entryViewController(coder:sender:segueIdentifier:)` with the following:

```
@IBSegueAction func entryViewController(coder: NSCoder,
  sender: Any?, segueIdentifier: String?) ->
  UINavigationController? {
    guard let cell = sender as? EntryTableViewCell,
      let indexPath = tableView.indexPath(for: cell),
      let navigationController
        = UINavigationController(coder: coder),
      let entryTableViewController
        = navigationController.topViewController as?
        EntryTableViewController else { return nil }
    entryTableViewController.entry
      = dataSource?.itemIdentifier(for: indexPath)
    self.entryTableViewController = entryTableViewController
    return navigationController
}
```

It's important to understand that an `NSCoder` gets passed into this function, where it's used to initialize the navigation controller found in the storyboard. Notice that once the navigation controller is initialized, an **EntryTableViewController** is already the `topViewController`.

Back in **Main.storyboard**, open the Library and add a **Split View Controller** to the canvas. Delete the following scenes from the canvas attached to the split view controller:

- **Navigation Controller**

- **Root View Controller**

- **View Controller**

Next, control-drag from the split view controller to the navigation controller attached to the Journalyst scene, and select **master view controller**. Then, connect the split view controller to the navigation controller of the entry table view scene, and select **detail view controller**.

Finally, select the split view controller scene and in the **Attributes inspector**, set the following properties:

- **Is Initial View Controller**

- **Style** is set to **Double Column**. This is required as of Xcode 12 to indicate whether your app supports a two or three column style app.

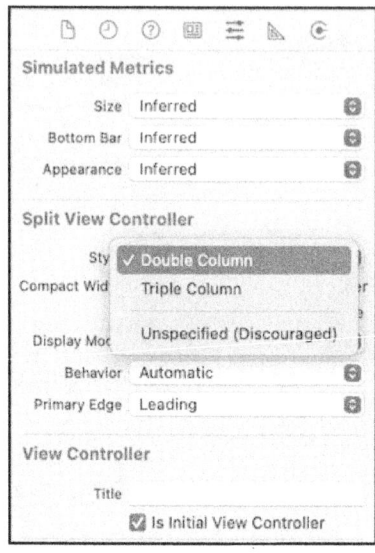

You're almost there!

In **AppDelegate.swift,** add the following to the end of the file:

```swift
// MARK: - Split view
extension AppDelegate: UISplitViewControllerDelegate {
  func splitViewController(
    _ splitViewController: UISplitViewController,
    collapseSecondary secondaryViewController: UIViewController,
    onto primaryViewController: UIViewController) -> Bool {
    guard let secondaryNavigationController
      = secondaryViewController as? UINavigationController,
      let entryTableViewController
        = secondaryNavigationController.topViewController
        as? EntryTableViewController else {
          return false
    }
    if entryTableViewController.entry == nil {
      return true
    }
    return false
  }
}
```

This conforms **AppDelegate** to `UISplitViewControllerDelegate`. Here, it is simply configuring the behavior of how the split view controller will handle the view on the right hand side of the controller.

Last, add the code below to the main body of **AppDelegate**:

```
func application(_ application: UIApplication,
  didFinishLaunchingWithOptions launchOptions:
  [UIApplication.LaunchOptionsKey: Any]?) -> Bool {
    if let window = window,
      let splitViewController
        = window.rootViewController as? UISplitViewController {
          splitViewController.preferredDisplayMode = .automatic
          splitViewController.delegate = self
    }
    return true
}
```

Here, you set the `preferredDisplayMode` of split view controller to automatic. This wraps up the work needed to get your split view controller to work.

Build and run your app, and you should see it is updated with a split view controller!

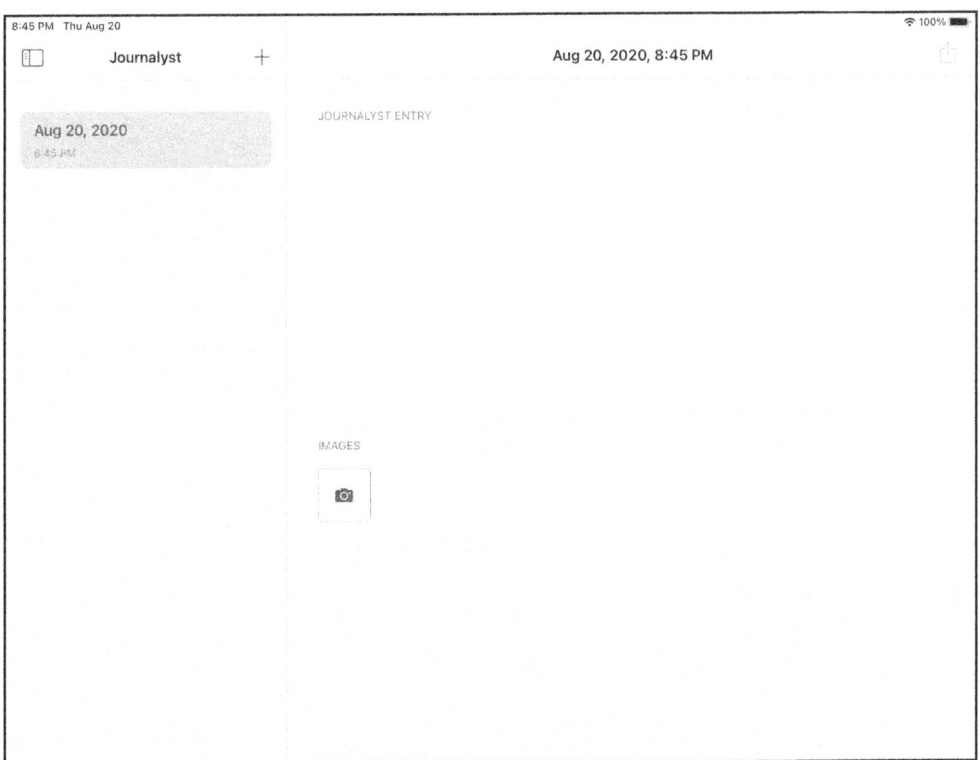

Updating the UI

Even though you have a working split view controller, you'll notice that not everything is working smoothly. The first entry in the list does not automatically get shown in the **EntryTableViewController**. To get that working, open **MainTableViewController.swift** and add this code to `viewDidLoad()`:

```
if let splitViewController = splitViewController,
  let splitNavigationController
    = splitViewController.viewControllers.last
    as? UINavigationController,
  let topViewController
    = splitNavigationController.topViewController
    as? EntryTableViewController {
  entryTableViewController = topViewController
}
```

This will give the view controller access to the **EntryViewController** present on the right side of the screen.

Next, replace `populateMockData()` with the following:

```
private func populateMockData() {
  reloadSnapshot(animated: false)
  if let entryTableViewController = entryTableViewController,
    let entry = entries.first,
    entryTableViewController.entry == nil {
    tableView.selectRow(at: IndexPath(row: 0, section: 0),
                        animated: false,
                        scrollPosition: .top)
    entryTableViewController.entry = entry
  }
}
```

Now, whenever the data is initially loaded, the first entry in the table view will get selected automatically.

Build and run everything again. You should see the time of the first entry appear at the top of the **EntryTableViewController** navigation controller.

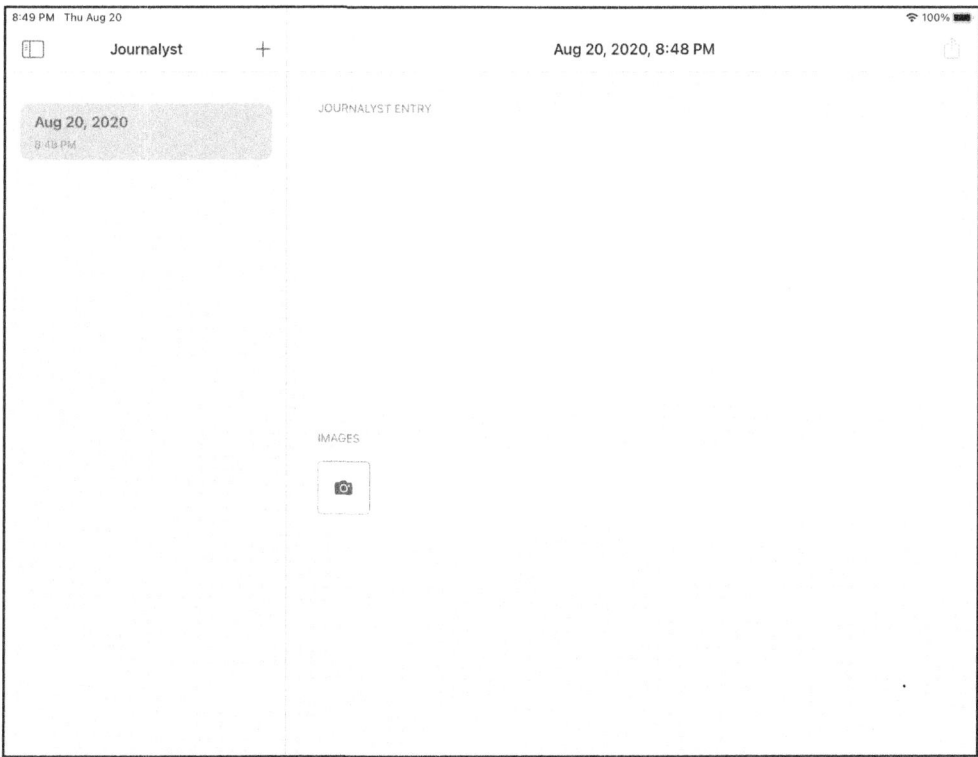

We're getting close, but there are still a few more pieces to consider. Currently, text added to an entry doesn't save, and adding an entry image or trying to share an entry causes a crash.

Open **EntryTableViewController.swift** and add the following method to the UITextViewDelegate extension:

```
func textViewDidEndEditing(_ textView: UITextView) {
  entry?.log = textView.text
}
```

Now, when you switch entries in the left-hand side, the text contained in the text view will be saved to the entry you were previously editing.

Next, you need to fix image and sharing functionality. When the app is running on an iPhone, the system will handle showing the activity controller and action sheet for you. However, on iPad you need to do a little more for it to work.

Because iPad wants to present the action sheet in a `UIPopoverPresentationController`, you'll need to tell it where to present from. In `addImage(_:)`, add the following just before the last line of the method:

```
if let sender = sender,
  let popoverController =
  actionSheet.popoverPresentationController {
  popoverController.sourceRect = CGRect(x: sender.frame.midX,
                                        y: sender.frame.midY,
                                        width: 0,
                                        height: 0)
  popoverController.sourceView = sender
}
```

Here, you check if there is a popover presentation controller, and then set the `sourceRect` and `sourceView` properties. Now, when you tap the camera button, the modal will be presented from it.

Last, add the following in `share(_:)`. Once again, place this code just before the last line:

```
if let popoverController =
    activityController.popoverPresentationController {
    popoverController.barButtonItem =
    navigationItem.rightBarButtonItem
}
```

While very similar to the previous additions for `addImage(_:)`, in this case, the share button is in a navigation bar. Therefore, you simply set the `barButtonItem` of the popoverController. Now, both modals will work properly.

Build and run the app. Now, try adding some text to a journal entry, add a few images and try to share.

Everything should be in working order:

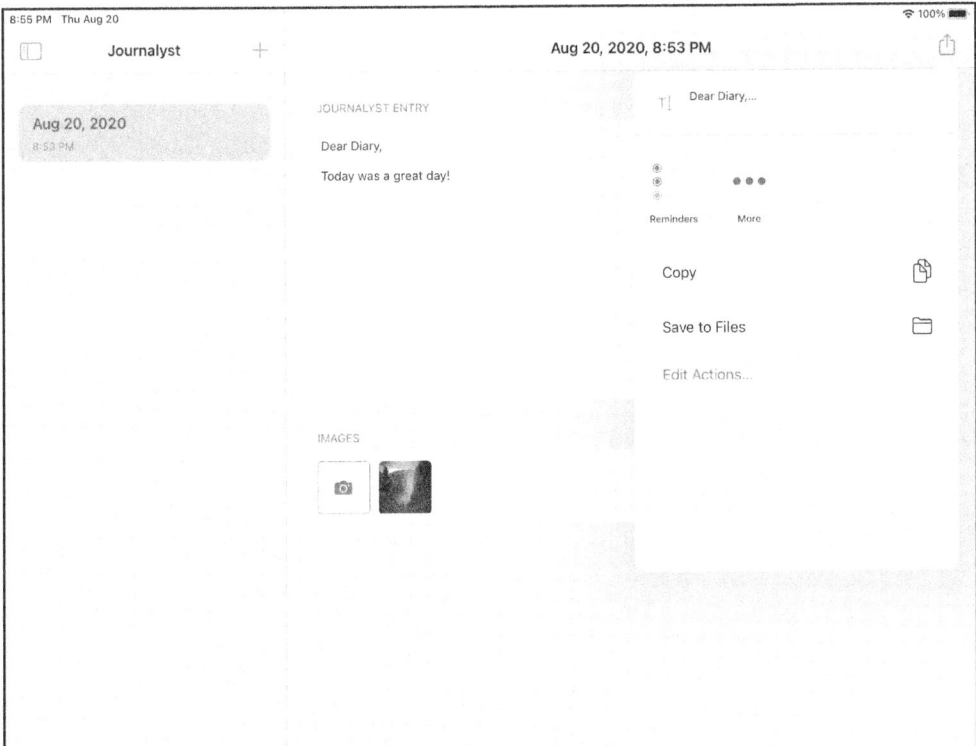

macOS split views

In traditional macOS apps, split views have long been the standard way of presenting a UI in a similar way to the split view controller. Catalyst makes it easy to take a split view controller and turn it into something that looks right at home on a Mac.

To see what the app looks like on a Mac, change the device in your active scheme to **My Mac**, then build and run the app again and add a few more journal entries:

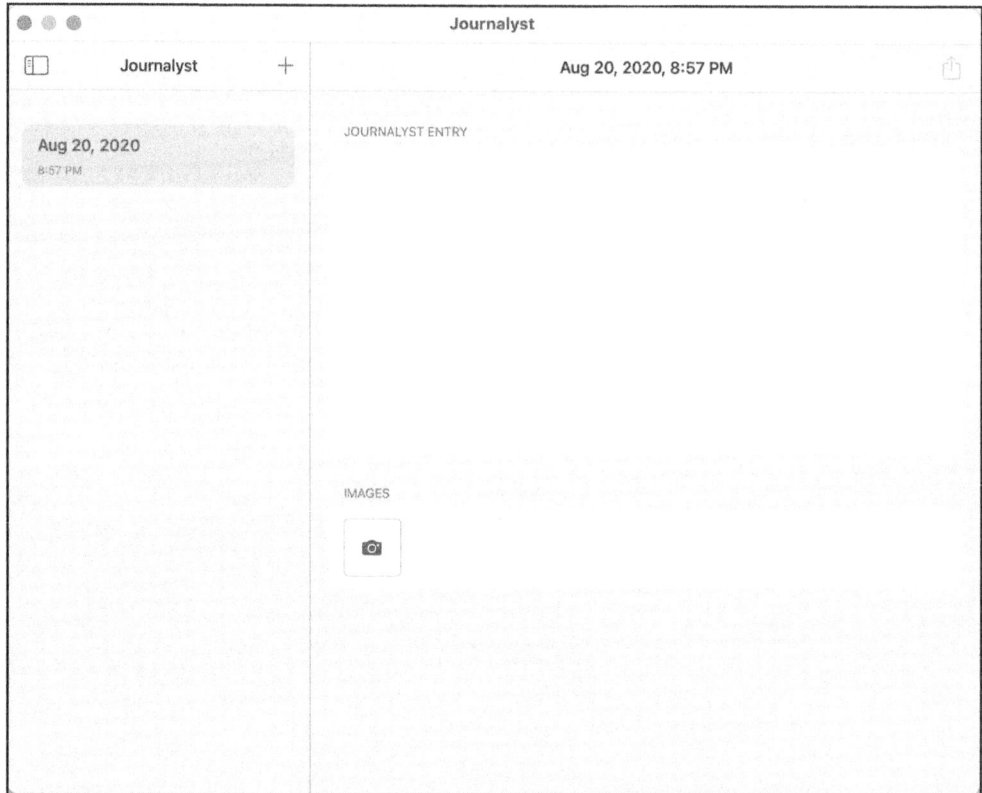

You should see the app looks almost exactly the same as it did on iPad.

> **Note**: Don't forget to set your team in your project's settings for **Signing & Capabilities**.

There are a few pieces of the user interface that aren't quite right, like the entry table view. Typically, the side views on Mac have some transparency. The first thing you can do to address this is set the split view controller's primary background style.

Open **AppDelegate.swift** and add the following to the end of the if let block, right after setting splitViewController.delegate:

```
splitViewController.primaryBackgroundStyle = .sidebar
```

This style will not have any affect on iPad or iPhone apps, but will make your app feel much more at home on a Mac.

Build and run one last time, and again, add a few entries. You'll see there's a much better look and feel now:

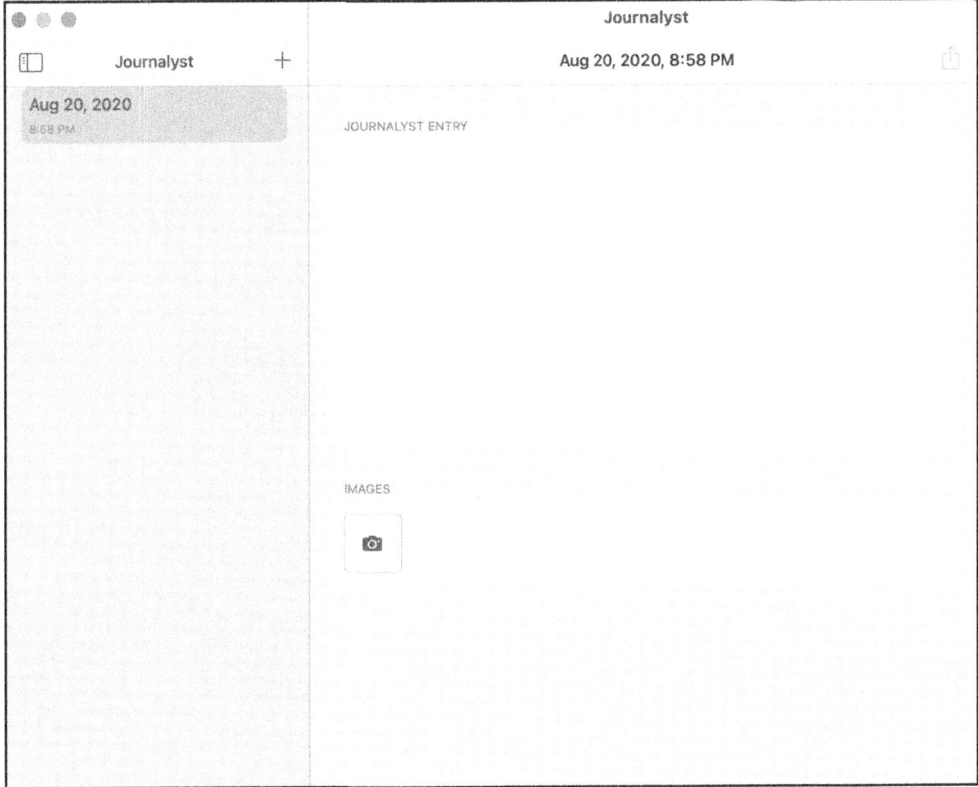

Key points

- Split view controllers make it easy to create an iOS and macOS app from the same codebase.

- Popovers on iPadOS and macOS are handled identically.

- There is minimal work to make a split view controller look proper on macOS.

Where to go from here?

This chapter got you from an iPhone-only app to a working iPad and macOS app that feels right at home on each platform. You learned what changes you need to make to handle the different platforms, and how much Catalyst will handle for you.

You can learn more about the following subjects here:

- **UISplitViewController**: https://developer.apple.com/documentation/uikit/uisplitviewcontroller

- **IBSegueAction**: https://developer.apple.com/videos/play/wwdc2019/210/

- **Catalyst**: https://developer.apple.com/design/human-interface-guidelines/ios/overview/ipad-apps-for-mac/

Chapter 3: Drag & Drop

By Marin Benčević

On macOS, dragging and dropping files is such an integral feature that we typically just take its presence for granted. It's so useful that Apple decided to bring it over to the iPad in iOS 11. With Catalyst, you can go full circle and bring the iPad's drag and drop *back* to macOS. Everything old is new again, right?

In this chapter, you'll update the app you've been working on so your users can add new photos to their diary entry by dragging them from other apps and dropping them into the entry view. You'll also update the entry photos collection view to allow reordering the photos by dragging and dropping.

How do drag and drop work?

Before you start working, you need to get familiar with the basics of drag and drop. I know theory can be *a drag*, but bear with me here.

Each drag and drop action has two sides: The dragging side and the dropping side. The objects on both of these sides are UIViews. To enable dragging, you need to add a **drag interaction** to a view. When iOS detects that a drag is being attempted on a view, the drag interaction uses a **drag interaction delegate** to determine which **drag items** will be dragged. This delegate can also customize the look of these items as they're being dragged.

The whole point of drag and drop is to share data between apps. The **drag items** being passed around are not the actual data. Instead, they contain a way to *get* the data once the drop happens.

On the other side, a **drop interaction** uses a **drop interaction delegate** to determine what will happen when the item is dropped into the destination view. The drop interaction delegate can also animate the destination view whenever the dragged items enter the destination view or change position inside the view.

Overseeing all of this is a **drop session**. Drop session is a manager, but the good kind of manager: It lets you work without getting in your way, but always has answers ready to any pressing questions you might have. The session knows which items are being dragged, how to get their contents, where they're being dropped to and other useful contextual information.

To enable drag and drop on your views, all you need to do is add the interactions and implement the delegate methods. Once you do that for your iPad app, it will work on macOS automatically. It also works on iOS, but only inside your app.

OK, that's the theory. Let's *drop* right in and get into some code!

Dropping new photos

Open the starter project from the provided materials and run it on an iPad. Take a look at the entry photos collection view. Currently, you can only add new photos by clicking on the camera icon and choosing a photo. On macOS and the iPad, it's common to select a bunch of photos from the Photos app and just drop them into the destination app. Let's make that happen.

Before you can start working on drag and drop, there are a few project-specific changes you need to make. When the app loads, it first launches the *main* table view controller, which in turn creates a new *entry* table view controller with a new entry. At the time of writing, in some cases, the split view controller will only load the *entry* table view controller, without loading the master. In those cases, the entry will be `nil`. To work around this issue, you'll force the app to always perform some setup after it launches.

Open **MainTableViewController.swift** and add a new method to the class:

```
func prepareForPresentation() {
  loadViewIfNeeded()
  populateMockData()
}
```

This method will perform the necessary setup actions that populate your app with an empty entry.

Next, open **AppDelegate.swift** and add the following code at the end of the `if` block inside `application(_:didFinishLaunchingWithOptions:)`, right after where you set `primaryBackgroundStyle`:

```
if let mainNavigationController =
  splitViewController.viewController(for: .primary)
  as? UINavigationController,
  let mainViewController =
  mainNavigationController.viewControllers.first
  as? MainTableViewController {
    mainViewController.prepareForPresentation()
}
```

The above code fetches the main table view controller and calls the method you added earlier every time the app launches. This makes sure entry table view controller always has an entry to work with.

With that out of the way, you can get started on dropping photos into the app!

Open **EntryTableViewController.swift** and at the bottom of `viewDidLoad` add the following code:

```
let interaction = UIDropInteraction(delegate: self)
textView.interactions.append(interaction)
```

As mentioned before, for dropping to work you need to add a `UIDropInteraction` to a view. In this case, you'll allow dropping photos inside the text view of the entry screen.

Next, at the bottom of the file, add the following extension to implement
UIDropInteractionDelegate:

```
// MARK: - Drop Interaction Delegate
extension EntryTableViewController:
  UIDropInteractionDelegate {
  func dropInteraction(
    _ interaction: UIDropInteraction,
    canHandle session: UIDropSession) -> Bool {
    session.canLoadObjects(ofClass: UIImage.self)
  }
}
```

As you enable drag and drop, you need to first declare the kinds of things that can be
dropped inside the view. In this case, you'll only accept the drop if the session has at
least one drag item that's a UIImage.

Now implement the following method inside the extension:

```
func dropInteraction(
  _ interaction: UIDropInteraction,
  sessionDidUpdate session: UIDropSession) -> UIDropProposal {
  UIDropProposal(operation: .copy)
}
```

As items are dragged inside a view, this method is called repeatedly. This method
returns a **proposal** of what *could* happen if the user were to drop the items right now.
In the proposal, you define what kind of drop operation this would be with a value
from the UIDropOperation enumeration. In this case, you return .copy which
means that the dropped item will be copied from the source app to your app, and the
user will see a "+" sign while dropping.

Other possible values of this enumeration include:

- .move: Tells the user that the item will be moved.

- .cancel: Says that the drag will be canceled.

- .forbidden: Used when the drop is *usually* enabled for this view, but there's
  something about the combination of dragged items and destination view's state
  forbidding this in a specific case.

> **Note**: During a drag interaction, `dropInteraction(_:sessionDidUpdate:)` gets called many, *many* times. Make sure you're not doing any long-lasting work in there.

The last piece of the puzzle is to define what happens once the user drops the dragged items. Add the following method inside the `UIDropInteractionDelegate` extension:

```
func dropInteraction(
  _ interaction: UIDropInteraction,
  performDrop session: UIDropSession) {
  session.loadObjects(ofClass: UIImage.self) {
    [weak self] imageItems in
    guard let self = self else { return }
  }
}
```

This method gets called when the user releases the dragged items into the view. To get the dragged photos, you can ask the session to load all the dragged items of type `UIImage`.

Once the images are loaded you can add them to the entry and update the collection view. Add the following code inside the closure:

```
if let images = imageItems as? [UIImage] {
  self.entry?.images.insert(contentsOf: images, at: 0)
}
self.reloadSnapshot(animated: true)
```

Here, you're casting the received array to `[UIImage]`. Once you have the photos, you prepend them to the entry and add a number of items at the start of the collection view equal to the number of photos that were just dropped. `reloadSnapshot` will automatically animate the changes you make to the collection view's data source.

> **Note**: `loadObjects` can only be called inside this delegate method. You can't access a drag item's data before or after this point. The completion handler is always called on the main queue, so there's no need to use dispatch here.

Build and run the project on an iPad. The easiest devices to test on are 11-inch or larger iPad Pros. Enter split-screen with **Photos** by dragging the icon to the right-hand side of the screen. Find some nice vacation photos and drag the photos over to the **text view** of the entry screen:

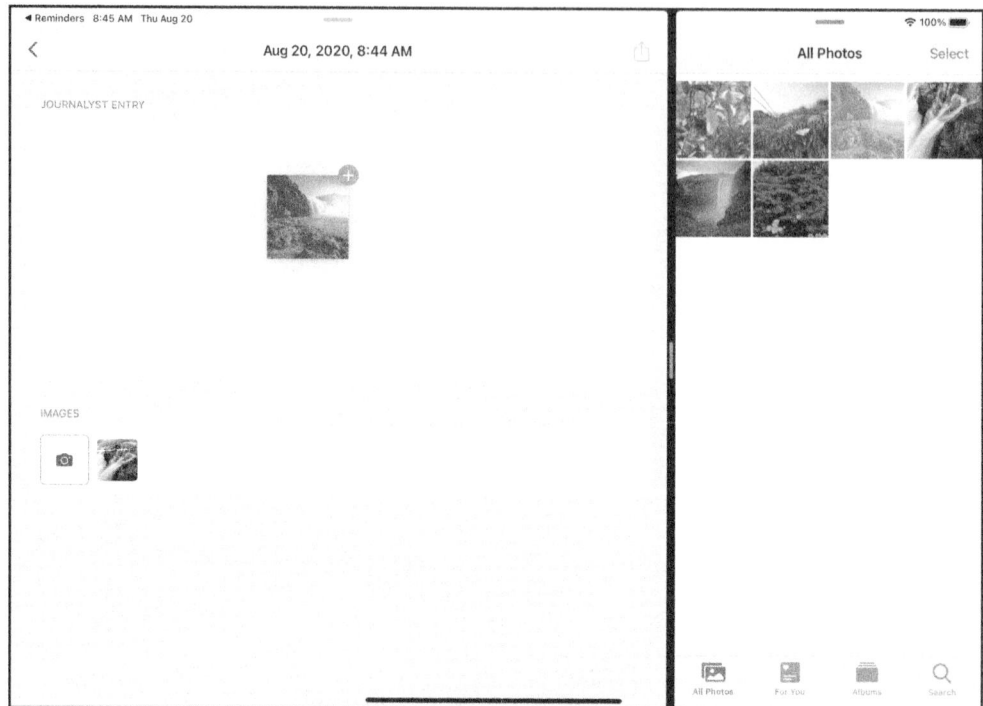

You should see the photos appear in the collection view:

Dropping photos like this is much easier than going through an image picker and looking for the perfect photo. Now that the user can drop photos into the text view, let's allow them to drop photos directly into the collection view.

Dropping inside UICollectionView

Dropping photos in the text view is convenient when you want to add a bunch of photos to the entry, but it would be nice to let the users drag photos into specific positions directly inside the collection view. You'll also show an animation of the existing photos parting to allow space for the newly dropped photos.

Thankfully, UIKit includes drag and drop APIs specific to table and collection views. While you will work on adding drag and drop to a collection view, the same process is valid for table views with minor method name changes.

Still in **EntryTableViewController.swift**, start by adding the following line to the end of `viewDidLoad`:

```
collectionView.dropDelegate = self
```

`UICollectionViewDropDelegate` is very similar to the delegate you implemented earlier in this chapter, except it has additional features specific to collection views.

Add the following extension to the bottom of the file to implement the delegate:

```
// MARK: - Collection View Drop Delegate
extension EntryTableViewController:
  UICollectionViewDropDelegate {
  func collectionView(
    _ collectionView: UICollectionView,
    canHandle session: UIDropSession) -> Bool {
    session.canLoadObjects(ofClass: UIImage.self)
  }
}
```

This is the same implementation as before. You're only interested in `UIImage` instances.

Next, implement the following method in the extension:

```
func collectionView(
  _ collectionView: UICollectionView,
  dropSessionDidUpdate session: UIDropSession,
  withDestinationIndexPath destinationIndexPath: IndexPath?)
  -> UICollectionViewDropProposal {
  UICollectionViewDropProposal(
    operation: .copy,
    intent: .insertAtDestinationIndexPath)
}
```

This method, like the one you implemented before, returns a proposal. For collection views, there's one additional piece of information: The **drop proposal intent**. The intent defines what would happen to the collection view if the user dropped the items right now.

You return `.insertAtDestinationIndexPath` which makes the collection view part the items to the left and right of the cursor, and show an empty space where the dragged items will be dropped. This signals to the user that the items will be dropped at that specific position.

Another possible value of this enumeration is `.insertIntoDestinationIndexPath`. This tells the user that the dropped items will be dropped *inside* the cell. This is useful for things like nested cells or cells that contain items inside of them.

Finally, implement the method that performs the actual drop:

```
func collectionView(
  _ collectionView: UICollectionView,
  performDropWith coordinator:
  UICollectionViewDropCoordinator) {
  let destinationIndex = coordinator.destinationIndexPath ??
    IndexPath(item: 0, section: 0)
}
```

A difference between the delegate you implemented earlier and this one is that the collection view delegate gets a **collection view drop coordinator**. This coordinator has a reference to the drop session, but also includes collection view specific contextual information, like which index path the user is dropping to. You'll use this information to add photos to specific indices in the `entries` array.

Add the following code to the method:

```
// 1
coordinator.session.loadObjects(ofClass: UIImage.self) {
  [weak self] imageItems in
  guard let self = self else { return }
  if let images = imageItems as? [UIImage] {
    // 2
    self.entry?.images.insert(
      contentsOf: images,
      at: destinationIndex.item)
  }
  // 3
  self.reloadSnapshot(animated: true)
}
```

This code is similar to the one you wrote earlier from dropping into the text view. Here's what's going on:

1. First, ask the session to load all `UIImage` objects.

2. Then, insert those objects into the destination index you got above.

3. Once you update the array, just like before, you call `reloadSnapshot` to make sure that the collection view animates those changes.

Build and run the app. Drag over a few photos to the collection view.

Once you have at least one photo, when dragging another one across the collection view you'll notice the items move to show an empty space where the item will be dropped.

If you drop the item, it will animate into position. That's a pretty cool effect with no manual animation code. Thanks, UIKit!

Now that you have dropping in your collection view, why not add dragging as well? Read on to find out how!

Reordering collection view items

Speaking of the work UIKit does for you, if you implement both dragging and dropping for a collection or table view, it will automatically support reordering the elements. That's why your next task is adding drag support to the collection view. By the end of this section, you'll be a real drag queen!

Add the following line to `viewDidLoad`:

```
collectionView.dragDelegate = self
```

Just like there's a collection view specific drop delegate, there's also a drag delegate. Begin the implementation of the protocol with the following extension at the bottom of the file:

```
// MARK: - Collection View Drag Delegate
extension EntryTableViewController:
  UICollectionViewDragDelegate {
  func collectionView(
    _ collectionView: UICollectionView,
    itemsForBeginning session: UIDragSession,
    at indexPath: IndexPath) -> [UIDragItem] {
    guard let entry = entry, !entry.images.isEmpty else {
      return []
    }
    let image = entry.images[indexPath.item]
    let provider = NSItemProvider(object: image)
    return [UIDragItem(itemProvider: provider)]
  }
}
```

For dragging to work, there's only one required method you have to implement. This method gets called when UIKit detects a dragging interaction is about to begin, and it asks you for the items that are being dragged. Thankfully, the delegate method includes the dragged index path as a parameter, making the task of finding the image much easier.

You check that there *is* an image to drag, and then get the image at that index path. If there is no image, you return an empty array, which stops the drag interaction and lets UIKit interpret the drag as a regular touch or mouse event.

Remember the item providers mentioned earlier? They define how data will be transferred from one app to the other. Some existing UIKit classes like `UIImage` already implement the required methods for this, so you can easily create a provider just by passing the image. Once you have the provider, you return an array that contains a drag item with that provider.

With the drag delegate implemented, you need to make a few changes to your existing code to support rearranging items. Change the implementation of `collectionView(_:dropSessionDidUpdate:withDestinationIndexPath:)` to the following code:

```
if session.localDragSession != nil {
  return UICollectionViewDropProposal(
      operation: .move,
      intent: .insertAtDestinationIndexPath)
} else {
  return UICollectionViewDropProposal(
```

```
        operation: .copy,
        intent: .insertAtDestinationIndexPath)
}
```

A **local drag session** is a drag session that was started inside your app. If the session is local, you return a `.move` drop operation because the items will be moved from one index path to another. If it's not a local session, you return `.copy` like before.

Next, when the user is rearranging items, you first need to delete the original item and then add it to its new position. Add the following lines to `collectionView(_:performDropWith:)`, right before the `loadObjects` call:

```
if coordinator.session.localDragSession != nil {
  for item in coordinator.items {
    guard let sourceIndex = item.sourceIndexPath else {
      return
    }
    self.entry?.images.remove(at: sourceIndex.item)
  }
}
```

If this is a local drag session, go through each item to be dropped. Each item contains a source index path, or the index path it was dragged from. You remove the dragged image from the source index in the images array. This ensures users don't accidentally duplicate items when trying to rearrange them.

Build and run. Like before, add a few photos to the collection view. Then try to drag one of the photos from the collection view to another position. You'll notice when you drag, it disappears from its original position, and a parting animation happens when you move over a different position. Once you drop it, the collection view animates it into that position:

You just made your app's user experience much better by allowing users to drag, drop and rearrange photos with a smooth look and feel, and all with minimal code.

And *guess what*, this works on macOS without any code changes. If you don't believe me, set the active scheme to **My Mac** and run the app. Find some vacation photos in the Finder and drag them over to the app.

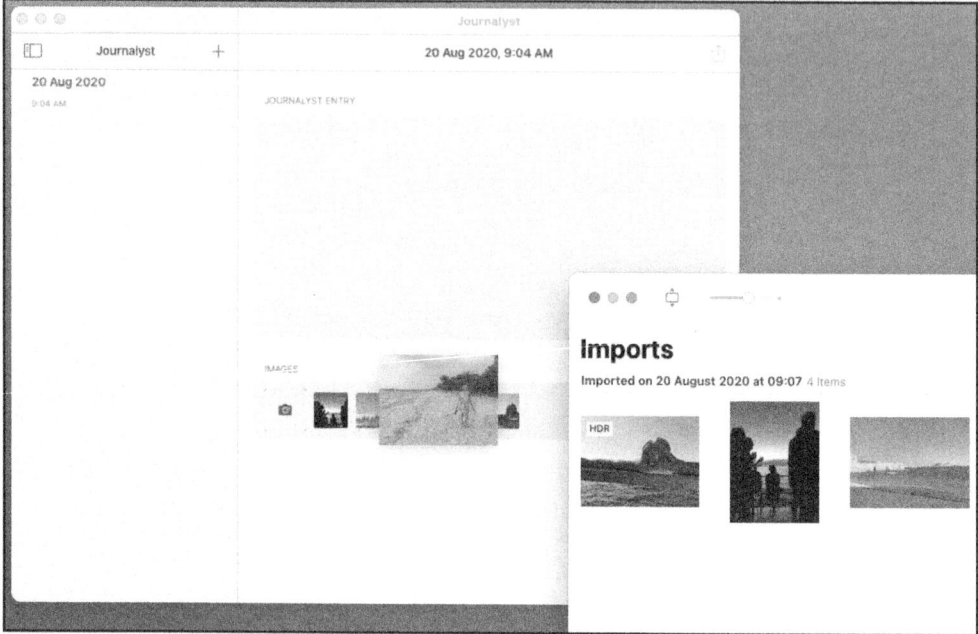

As a developer, there's nothing better than features working without any extra code. Now you know how to implement drag and drop! I only hope this chapter didn't *drag* on for too long.

Key points

- Add drag and drop to custom views by adding a **drag** or **drop interaction** to the view and implementing the necessary delegate methods.

- Use a **drag session** to get the dragged items and load the dragged data.

- For table and collection views, it's enough to implement the collection or table view specific drop and drag delegate methods.

- An iPadOS implementation of drag and drop works on macOS and iOS, but on iOS, it only works within one app.

Where to go from here?

In this chapter, you implemented a basic implementation of drag and drop. You can go even further by including custom animations while the user is dragging items across your views. You can also customize how item previews look while they're being dragged. You can see an implementation of that in the WWDC 2017 session called Mastering Drag and Drop which you can find here: apple.co/2vOhvYA.

For collection and table views, you can make the user interface smoother by utilizing placeholder cells. When the user is dragging over the table or collection view, you can show placeholder cells with loading indicators. Once the items are loaded, the cell gets updated. You can see this in action in the WWDC 2017 session called Drag and Drop with Collection and Table View, which you can find here: apple.co/2JzzTOw.

Chapter 4: Setting the Scene(s)

By Nick Bonatsakis

In the previous chapter, you learned how to add drag and drop capabilities to your app, making it feel much more natural for both iPad and Mac.

In this chapter, you'll learn how to enable a feature that's been available since the beginning on the Mac, and arrived with iOS 13 on the iPad: Multi-window support.

By the end of this chapter, you'll have learned:

- What multi-window support is and why you'd want to enable it for your app.

- How to enable basic multi-window support in Xcode and in your app.

- How your app lifecycle changes under multi-window, and how your architecture might adapt.

- How to add custom support for drag and drop window creation.

Ready to dive into the exciting world of multiple windows? Awesome! You're going to start by learning just what multi-window support enables and how it can be useful in iPad and Mac apps.

Introducing multiple windows for iPad

In 2007, Apple unveiled the next generation of computing with the introduction of the iPhone. Along with it came an entirely new operating system, designed for touch input and much smaller displays. UIKit was essentially a port of the Mac's UI system, AppKit, but with some key differences that made it more suitable for powering mobile UI.

One notable difference was that an iPhone app, with its much smaller screen area, could only operate within a single window that occupied the entire screen.

Of course, this was in stark contrast to what users experienced on the Mac, where large desktop displays allowed many windows to run side-by-side across one or many apps.

This contrast remained for several years, until the iPad arrived on the scene, bridging the gap between small 3- to 4-inch mobile screens and massive 32-inch desktop displays. Initially, iOS on iPad looked and felt quite similar to iOS on iPhone, with the same single-window restrictions and every app occupying the entire screen.

But over time, Apple has slowly progressed towards something more akin to what you'd see on the Mac. First, it added the ability to run apps side-by-side. Then it introduced tabs in apps like Safari. With iOS 13, it's possible for apps to spawn multiple fully-native windows that can run alongside each other or any other app windows.

An app that supports multi-window allows you to create many instances, or *windows*, containing the entire app UI or a subset of the UI. Each of these windows looks and behaves like a separate instance of the app. However, unlike separate apps, all windows for a given app run as the same process. You'll learn more about this later.

Why multi-window?

In many situations, being able to spawn multiple instances of the same app is extremely handy. Consider the following use-cases that are only possible with multi-window support:

- **Messages**: Carrying on two or more conversation threads without having to switch back and forth.

- **Pages**: Working on two documents side-by-side when you want to reference information in the first while working on the second and drag and drop content between the two.

- **Mail**: Writing a message in one window and searching previous messages for contacts or other information in the second window.

- **Safari**: Researching a topic across two different websites, side-by-side at the same time.

Generally, any app that lets a user view or create many instances of the same type of content is a good candidate for multi-window support.

Mac users, and now iPad users, will expect your app to function just as well, if not better, than the built-in Apple apps. If you want to build a first-class experience, take the time to enhance your app with support for multiple windows.

Multi-window in action

There are many ways to spawn and interact with multiple app windows on iPad. Some come with the system. Others are specific to individual apps. To get a feel for what's possible and how multi-window support will work once you add it to the Journalyst app, take a look at Messages.

Grab the nearest iPad or iPad Simulator and start by opening the Messages app. If you've ever used apps on the iPad in multi-tasking mode, where you run two different apps side-by-side, you'll know that you can swipe up from the bottom edge to reveal the dock. Go ahead and do so, then hold and drag the Messages icon to the right of the screen and drop it when you see the drop zone.

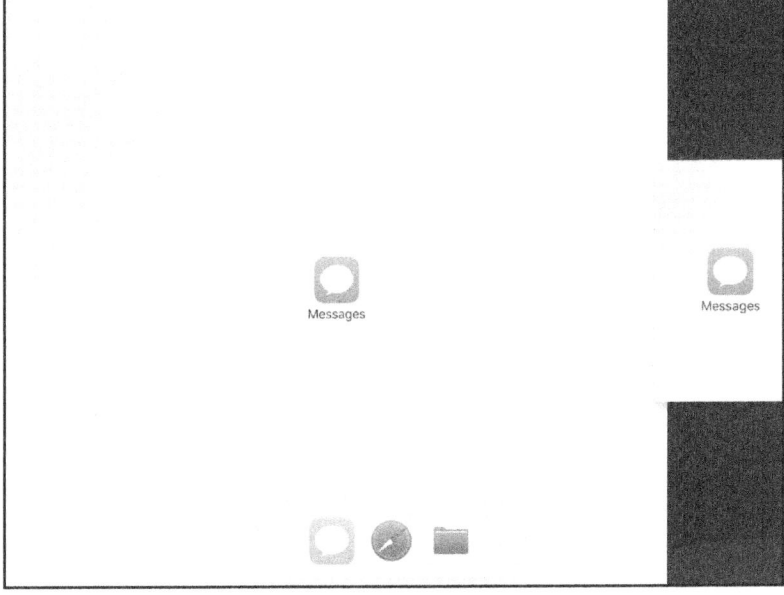

You now have Messages in a side-by-side split screen. Both windows are fully functional, as if you had two Messages apps running at once.

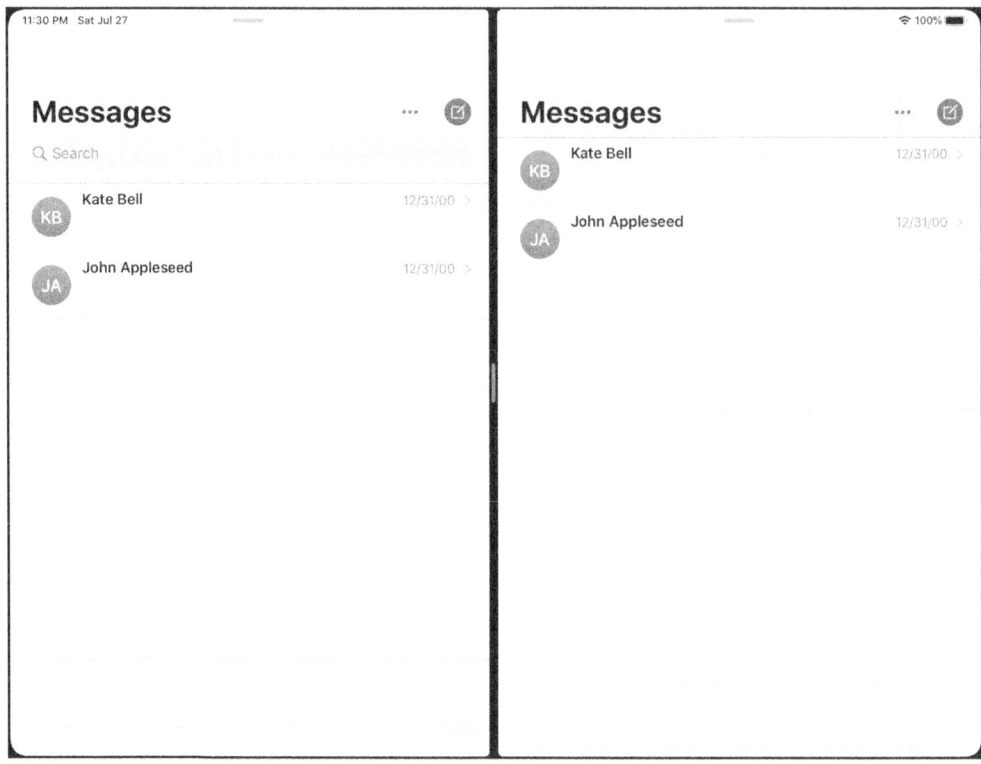

Notice the separator in the middle of the screen and the handle-looking control. Touch and hold on the handle and drag all the way to the right edge of the screen, seemingly dismissing the second window. But wait! You didn't dismiss that window, you just detached it into a fully separate window.

Swipe up from the bottom of the screen again to bring up the dock once more, then tap and hold on the Messages app icon until you see a contextual menu pop up. Tap on **Show All Windows** and you'll see a view of all the windows for this app, including the one you spawned and then swiped off to the right.

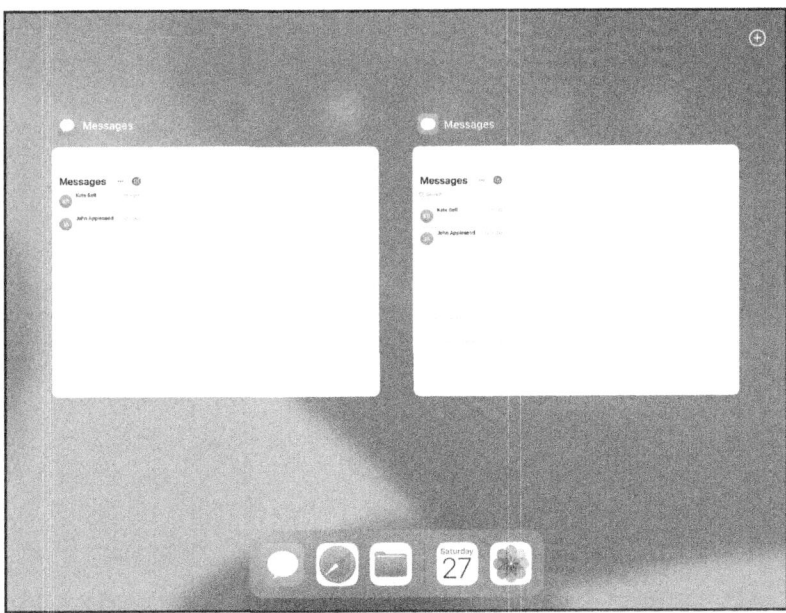

You'll notice here that there's also a "+" button you can use to create new windows. Try tapping it to see it in action.

Finally, tap on one of the windows to get back into Messages. Tap and hold on one of the conversations in the sidebar for a moment, drag it to the right edge of the screen, then drop it once you see the drop zone indicator.

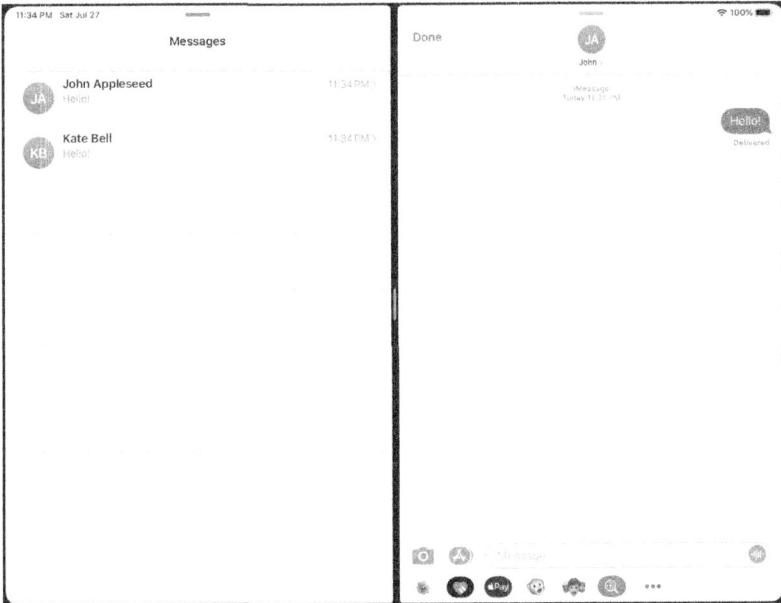

You should now see that conversation on the right side of the screen, while you still have a fully functioning Messages app on the left. The other multi-window controls are part of the baseline support, but this one needs some additional work because, as you might expect, the interaction is specific to the content in the Messages app.

If the idea of adding these features to Journalyst excites you (hint: It should), then strap in, because you're about to do just that!

Enabling multi-window in Xcode

Open the starter project for this chapter in Xcode and head over to the project settings. Click on the **Journalyst** target and make sure you're on the General tab. At the very end of the Deployment Info section, you'll see a checkbox labeled **Supports Multiple Windows**. Go ahead and check it to, you guessed it, enable multi-window support.

Now open **Info.plist** and you'll notice that Xcode has added a new entry, Application Scene Manifest. The dictionary contains only one sub-entry called **Enable Multiple Windows** and it's set to YES.

You might think this would be enough to add basic multi-window support. But if you were to run the app now, you'd see nothing but a big fat empty screen.

To understand why that is, you'll need to learn a bit about how the standard app architecture changes in a multi-window environment.

Introducing scenes

In the pre-multi-window world, the entry point to every app was the app delegate. Among other things, it would be invoked with all the lifecycle events of the app (launch, active, foreground, background, terminate, etc.). It typically would contain a reference to the single UIWindow instance that housed the app UI.

In an app that supports multi-window, the app delegate is still the main entry point. However, you can now have many windows, and you need to be able to manage and notify each of them of lifecycle events independently. To do all that, you need to add a new abstraction. That abstraction is called a **scene** and it has the following components:

- **Scene**: Represents a single instance of your app's UI, including basic information and state changes.

- **Scene Delegate**: Responds to state changes and events from a scene.

- **Scene Session**: Manages the scene process, including configuration and state restoration.

When you enable your app for multiple windows, the system will continue to invoke app-level lifecycle events such as didFinishLaunching and willTerminate on the app delegate. However, a scene will now handle all lifecycle events and information associated with an instance of your app's UI.

When you launch your app, the system will now create a scene session and its associated scene to represent the first instance of your app, much like it would create a single UIApplication instance for the entire app.

To respond to UI-instance-level lifecycle events, the system will now invoke a custom scene delegate implementation that you provide, much like your app delegate did previously. With each additional scene your user initiates, the system will create another instance of this stack, allowing your app to manage each of its windows independently.

Finish enabling multi-window

Now that you've learned how scenes allow you to effectively manage multiple instances of your app's UI, it's time to finish enabling multi-window support for your project.

Back in Xcode, create a new Swift file and name it **SceneDelegate.swift**, then add the following code:

```swift
import UIKit
class SceneDelegate: UIResponder, UIWindowSceneDelegate {
  var window: UIWindow?
  func scene(_ scene: UIScene,
    willConnectTo session: UISceneSession,
    options connectionOptions: UIScene.ConnectionOptions) {
    if let splitViewController =
          window?.rootViewController as?
          UISplitViewController {
          splitViewController.preferredDisplayMode =
          .oneBesideSecondary
    }
  }
}
```

There's not a lot going on in the above code, just a reference to the scene's UIWindow instance and the addition of scene(_:willConnectTo:options:). This gets called whenever you create a scene and connect it to the scene session. For now, that's all you need in the scene delegate. There's just one more thing you need to add before you're done with basic multi-window support.

Open **Info.plist** once more, copy the below snippet to the clipboard, then highlight the **Application Scene Manifest** entry. Then expand it and paste to add the new sub-entry.

```xml
<?xml version="1.0" encoding="UTF-8"?>
<!DOCTYPE plist PUBLIC "-//Apple//DTD PLIST 1.0//EN" "http://
www.apple.com/DTDs/PropertyList-1.0.dtd">
<plist version="1.0">
<dict>
    <key>UIWindowSceneSessionRoleApplication</key>
    <array>
        <dict>
            <key>UISceneConfigurationName</key>
            <string>Default Configuration</string>
            <key>UISceneDelegateClassName</key>
            <string>Journalyst.SceneDelegate</string>
            <key>UISceneStoryboardFile</key>
            <string>Main</string>
```

```
            </dict>
        </array>
    </dict>
    </plist>
```

If you expand the configuration fully, you'll see an Application Session Role that consists of an array of items, each containing the configuration for a particular scene type. In this case, there's only one entry in the list representing the default configuration that you use whenever you create a new scene. However, the app can define roles for specific window configurations. The following describes each key-value:

- **Configuration Name**: The identifier for this scene configuration.

- **Delegate Class Name**: The class that implements the scene delegate, which you'll use for an instance of this scene configuration.

- **Storyboard Name**: The name of the storyboard you'll use to create an instance of this scene.

With the above configuration change in place, build and run. Long press on the app icon, show all windows and you'll find that you can now use the system UI to create new windows.

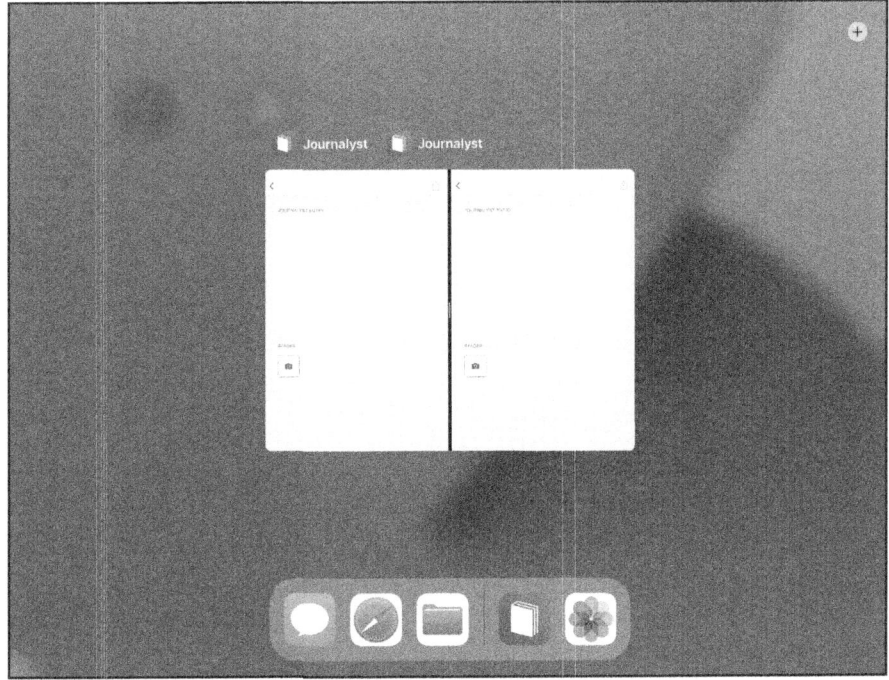

Things are looking great, but if you start playing with the app across several windows, you might start to notice that a few things are off. In particular, try bringing up the app in two side-by-side windows by revealing the dock and dragging the app icon to the right edge. Once you have both windows in place, go back to the main table view controller and try adding some new entries in the left window. Gasp! The right window's entry list doesn't change in the slightest.

Well, that's certainly a day-wrecker, but no worries! You're about to learn why this problem occurs and, more importantly, how to fix it.

Improving the standard multi-window experience

Remember that when iOS creates a new scene for your app, it's instantiating an entirely new and parallel instance of everything required to build your UI. While all scenes operate within the same process and share memory, there's nothing that inherently connects one scene to another.

Before you learn how to resolve the data issue that you introduced by moving to multi-window, you'll need to understand how the Journalyst app currently propagates data changes from its data layer to the UI layer when a user adds an entry.

Open **MainTableViewController.swift** and have a look at the addEntry method:

```
@IBAction private func addEntry(_ sender: Any) {
  DataService.shared.addEntry(Entry())
  reloadSnapshot(animated: true)
}
```

The above method gets called whenever you tap the **Add** button on the entries list sidebar. There's nothing overly complex going on here; you persist the entry to an in-memory data store via DataService.shared.addEntry and then call reloadSnapshot to refresh the UITableView state.

Now, open **DataService.swift** and take a peek at its addEntry method:

```
func addEntry(_ entry: Entry) {
  entries.append(entry)
}
```

Again, nothing too crazy here. You're just adding the new entry to the data service's internal data structure (in this case, an array).

The following diagram shows the data flow within each app scene; it should help clarify where the issue lies.

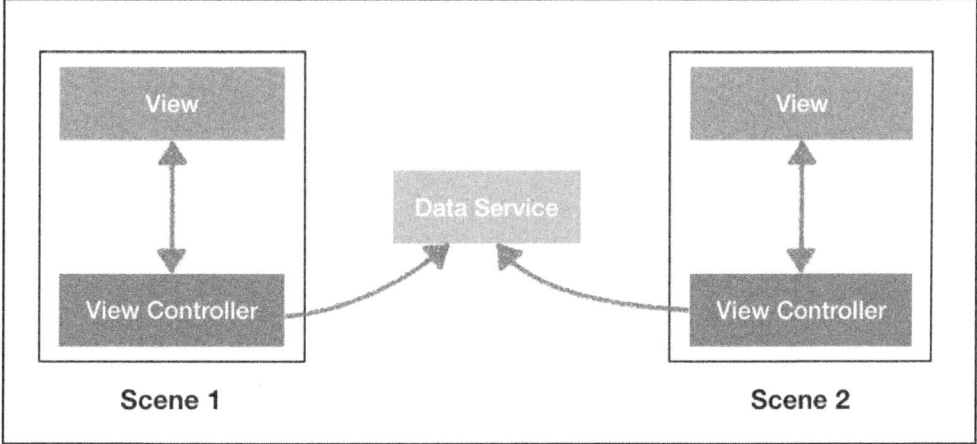

Here, you see that you're dealing with two identical, but entirely disconnected stacks. Data flows between the view controller and the view only within each separate scene. Data only flows into the Data Service, but not out. The view controller in the first scene initiates the adding of the entry and triggers the table refresh only in its own instance of MainTableViewController. Meanwhile, over in the second scene, there's an entirely separate instance of MainTableViewController that's never notified of the data change, and thus never reflects it.

Now that the data issue is apparent, you're going to write some code that will fix it. One common way to connect disparate components in an iOS or Mac app is through the use of Notifications and NotificationCenter. Here, you're going to leverage notifications to ensure that data changes get communicated across all scenes.

Start by opening **DataService.swift** and adding the following code before the DataService class definition:

```
extension Notification.Name {
  static var JournalEntriesUpdated
    = Notification.Name(
    "com.raywenderlich.Journalyst.EntriesUpdated")
}
```

The above code adds a new notification type by extending `Notification.Name` and adding the property `JournalEntriesUpdated`. This notification will be issued every time the data in any scene changes so that other scenes can observe and respond accordingly.

Next, modify `addEntry` and `removeEntry` to look like the following:

```
func addEntry(_ entry: Entry) {
  entries.append(entry)
  //1
  postUpdate()
}

func removeEntry(atIndex index: Int) {
  entries.remove(at: index)
  //2
  postUpdate()
}
```

And add the `postUpdate` method below:

```
private func postUpdate() {
  //3
  NotificationCenter.default.post(
    name: .JournalEntriesUpdated,
    object: nil)
}
```

Now, you're getting into some more meaty code, so take a moment to review what you did:

1. You call `postUpdate` to notify observers when the user adds new entries.

2. Next, you add the same `postUpdate` call to notify observers when the user removes entries.

3. Finally, you implement `postUpdate` by posting the notification you created earlier via `NotificationCenter`.

Great, now whenever the user adds or removes entries, this code will inform any observers of `JournalEntriesUpdated`. To close the loop, you'll need to subscribe to these updates in the appropriate places.

Open **MainTableViewController.swift** and start by removing the explicit calls to `reloadSnapshot` from `addEntry` and `tableView(_:trailingSwipeActionsConfigurationForRowAt:)` as follows:

```
@IBAction private func addEntry(_ sender: Any) {
```

```
    DataService.shared.addEntry(Entry())
  }

  override func tableView(
      _ tableView: UITableView,
      trailingSwipeActionsConfigurationForRowAt
      indexPath: IndexPath) -> UISwipeActionsConfiguration? {

    let deleteAction = UIContextualAction(
      style: .destructive,
      title: "Delete") {_, _, _ in
      DataService.shared.removeEntry(atIndex: indexPath.row)
    }

    deleteAction.image = UIImage(systemName: "trash")
    return UISwipeActionsConfiguration(actions: [deleteAction])
  }
```

You're about to drive UI updates by observing the data change notification you added, so you won't need to issue those updates explicitly anymore.

Next, add this code to the end of `viewDidLoad` to observe the data update notification.

```
  func viewDidLoad {
    ...
    //1
    NotificationCenter.default.addObserver(
      self,
      selector: #selector(handleEntriesUpdate),
      name: .JournalEntriesUpdated,
      object: nil)
  }
```

Then add `handleEntriesUpdate` to handle the change as follows:

```
  @objc func handleEntriesUpdate() {
    //2
    reloadSnapshot(animated: false)
  }
```

The above code adds the `MainTableViewController` as an observer. Specifically:

1. First, you subscribe to the `JournalEntriesUpdated` notification to receive updates whenever data changes.

2. Then, you call `reloadSnapshot(animated:)` whenever the notification handler triggers, to update the view.

Build and run, bring up the dock, and drag to create a side-by-side view once again.

Go back to main screen. Tap the **Add** button in either of the two scenes and watch in awe as the list in the other scene magically refreshes.

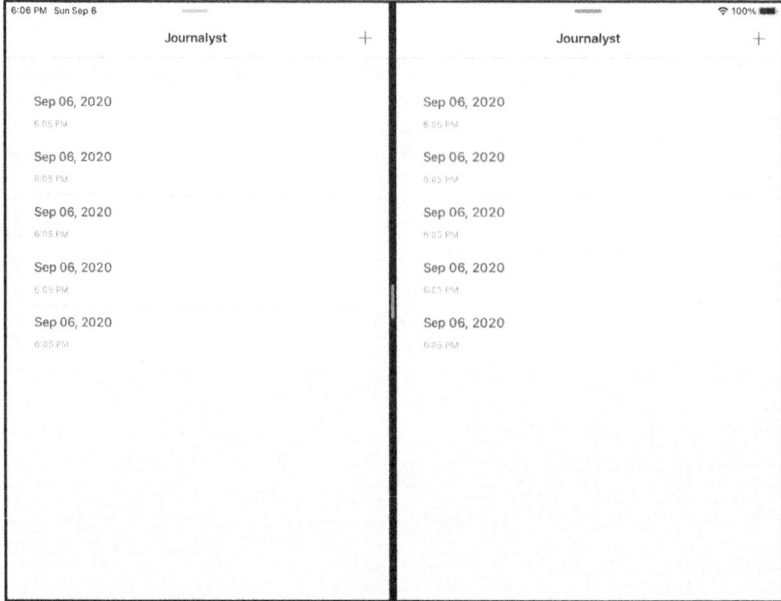

The app feels great now, so maybe you should go celebrate with a delicious dessert? Marzipan perhaps? Well, not so fast. There's still one more data issue lurking in your app that you'll need to address before kicking back with a treat.

With the app still running, enter some text on an entry in the first scene, then select a different entry. You'll notice that the cell for the entry updates with a preview of the text, but only in Scene 1.

To understand why this bug is happening, start by opening **EntryTableViewController.swift**. You'll notice this file includes the following delegate protocol declaration:

```
protocol EntryTableViewControllerDelegate: class {
  func entryTableViewController(
    _ controller: EntryTableViewController,
    didUpdateEntry entry: Entry)
}
```

If you look at viewWillDisappear(_:) in EntryTableViewController, you'll see that whenever this view controller disappears (e.g., leaves the screen), it notifies its delegate of the data change.

Open **MainTableViewController.swift** and have a look at the extension that
implements the `EntryTableViewControllerDelegate` interface:

```
// MARK: EntryTableViewControllerDelegate
extension MainTableViewController:
  EntryTableViewControllerDelegate {
  func entryTableViewController(
    _ controller: EntryTableViewController,
    didUpdateEntry entry: Entry) {
      reloadSnapshot(animated: false)
  }
}
```

In short, whenever the user updates an entry, the table view issues a snapshot reload
to ensure the list reflects the latest data. But once again, recall that changes specific
to a given view controller, or a group of view controller instances in one scene, do not
carry over to instances in other scenes.

So how might you fix this issue? Yup, the same way you fixed the first data problem:
By using notifications.

First things first, get rid of all references to `EntryTableViewControllerDelegate`,
including the extension and assignments in `MainTableViewController` and the
declaration and usages in **EntryTableViewController.swift**.

Next, open **DataService.swift** and change the `updateEntry(_:)` method to look like
this:

```
func updateEntry(_ entry: Entry) {
  //1
  var hasChanges = false
  entries = entries.map { item -> Entry in
    if item.id == entry.id && item != entry {
      //2
      hasChanges = true
      return entry
    } else {
  return item
    }
  }
  //3
  if hasChanges {
    postUpdate()
  }
}
```

Reviewing the changes you made:

1. First, you add a flag to track whether the provided entry represents an update or not.

2. You then track when it detects an entry change by assigning a value to `hasChanges`.

3. Finally, if it did detect a data change, you issue a data change notification by calling `postUpdate()`.

Since you are already handling the data change notification in `MainTableViewController`, that's all you have to do.

Build and run the app one more time. Go back to main screen on both sides. Try changing an entry in one scene while watching the list in the second scene. As soon as you leave the entry screen on **Scene 1**, you'll see the list preview for that entry updated in **Scene 2**.

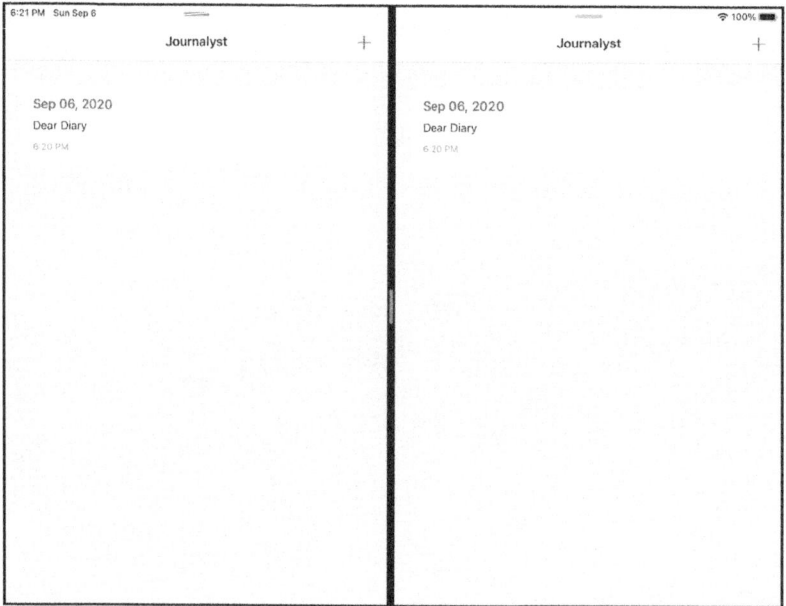

Nicely done! Your Journalyst app now has solid support for basic multi-windowing. But you're not one to settle for "basic", so you're going to implement one more feature that will take the scene support in this app to the next level.

Adding custom drag behavior to create a new window

Recall that when you explored multi-window support in the Messages app at the beginning of this chapter, you tried out a custom mechanism for spawning new scenes. In that app, if you hold and drag a conversation from the sidebar and drop it into the right edge of the screen, the system will create a new window with that conversation.

If you thought that interaction was pretty nifty, then you're in luck, because you're about to add it to Journalyst. When you're done, you'll be able to similarly hold, drag and drop a journal entry from the sidebar to start a new window with that entry's detail.

Start by opening **Entry.swift** and adding the following extension:

```
// MARK: NSUserActivity
extension Entry {
  //1
  static let OpenDetailActivityType
    = "com.raywenderlich.EntryOpenDetailActivityType"
  static let OpenDetailIdKey = "entryID"
  //2
  var openDetailUserActivity: NSUserActivity {
    //3
    let userActivity
      = NSUserActivity(activityType:
      Entry.OpenDetailActivityType)
    //4
    userActivity.userInfo = [Entry.OpenDetailIdKey: id]
    return userActivity
  }
}
```

The above code adds some functionality to `Entry` around `NSUserActivity`:

1. First, you declare several static properties for various identifiers you'll use later.

2. Next, you declare a computed property for an `NSUserActivity` that represents opening the detail screen for a journal entry.

3. You initialize the activity with the unique identifier you declared earlier.

4. Finally, you store the ID for the journal entry you want to show when you spawn a new window via this activity in `userInfo`.

Next, you need to add the drag behavior that initiates the interaction, so open
MainTableViewController.swift and add the following extension:

```
// MARK: UITableViewDragDelegate
extension MainTableViewController: UITableViewDragDelegate {
  //1
  func tableView(_ tableView: UITableView,
    itemsForBeginning session: UIDragSession,
    at indexPath: IndexPath) -> [UIDragItem] {
    //2
    let entry = DataService.shared.allEntries[indexPath.row]
    let userActivity = entry.openDetailUserActivity
    //3
    let itemProvider = NSItemProvider()
    itemProvider.registerObject(userActivity, visibility: .all)
    //4
    let dragItem = UIDragItem(itemProvider: itemProvider)
    return [dragItem]
  }
}
```

The above code might look a bit unfamiliar, so here's a breakdown of what it does:

1. `UITableViewDragDelegate` gets called when a drag interaction begins and
   allows you to specify the content involved in the operation.

2. Here, you fetch the `Entry` object that the user has long pressed on and use
   `entry.openDetailUserActivity` to obtain an `NSUserActivity` representative
   of that entry.

3. Next, you create an instance of `NSItemProvider` and register the user activity
   object.

4. Then you create a drag item with the item provider and return it. This will
   ultimately expose the user activity to the system when the user drags the entry to
   the edge of the screen.

Now, you'll need to declare `MainTableViewController` as the drag delegate for the
table view. Add the following code to the end of `viewDidLoad` to accomplish this:

```
tableView.dragDelegate = self
```

The last thing you need to do to enable your custom drag window interaction is to
handle the incoming user activity in the scene delegate. You do this by configuring
the new scene based on the provided entry ID.

Open **SceneDelegate.swift** and replace the entire implementation with the following:

```swift
import UIKit
class SceneDelegate: UIResponder, UIWindowSceneDelegate {
  var window: UIWindow?
  func scene(_ scene: UIScene,
    willConnectTo session: UISceneSession,
    options connectionOptions: UIScene.ConnectionOptions) {
    if let splitViewController
      = window?.rootViewController as? UISplitViewController {
        splitViewController.preferredDisplayMode
        = .oneBesideSecondary
    }
    //1
    if let userActivity
      = connectionOptions.userActivities.first {
      //2
      if !configure(window: window, with: userActivity) {
        print("Failed to restore from \(userActivity)")
      }
    }
  }

  func configure(window: UIWindow?,
    with activity: NSUserActivity) -> Bool {
    //3
    guard activity.activityType == Entry.OpenDetailActivityType,
      let entryID
        = activity.userInfo?[Entry.OpenDetailIdKey] as? String,
      let entry = DataService.shared.entry(forID: entryID),
      let entryDetailViewController
        = EntryTableViewController.loadFromStoryboard(),
      let splitViewController
        = window?.rootViewController
        as? UISplitViewController else {
      return false
    }

    //4
    entryDetailViewController.entry = entry
    //5
    let navController
      = UINavigationController(
      rootViewController: entryDetailViewController)
    splitViewController.showDetailViewController(
      navController, sender: self)
    return true
  }
}
```

That's quite a lot of code, so walk through it, step by step:

1. First, you check the `connectionOptions` for the presence of user activity. In the previous section, you configured the drag interaction to expose an `NSUserActivity` containing information about the target journal entry; here, you'll receive this activity.

2. Next, you call `configure`, passing the window and the user activity, and log a message in the case of failure.

3. Inside `configure`, you start by ensuring that the activity type matches `Entry.OpenDetailActivityType`. You then obtain the entry object, instantiate an instance of `EntryTableViewController` for displaying the entry and obtain a reference to the main split view controller.

4. You now configure the entry view controller to display the obtained entry object.

5. Lastly, you wrap the entry view controller in a navigation controller and present the navigation controller as the split view controller's detail content.

Now, when you drag and drop an entry on the edge of the screen, the system will relay your user activity, housed in the drag item, to the scene delegate. There, it will configure and present the entry detail immediately.

Go ahead and build and run to give it a try.

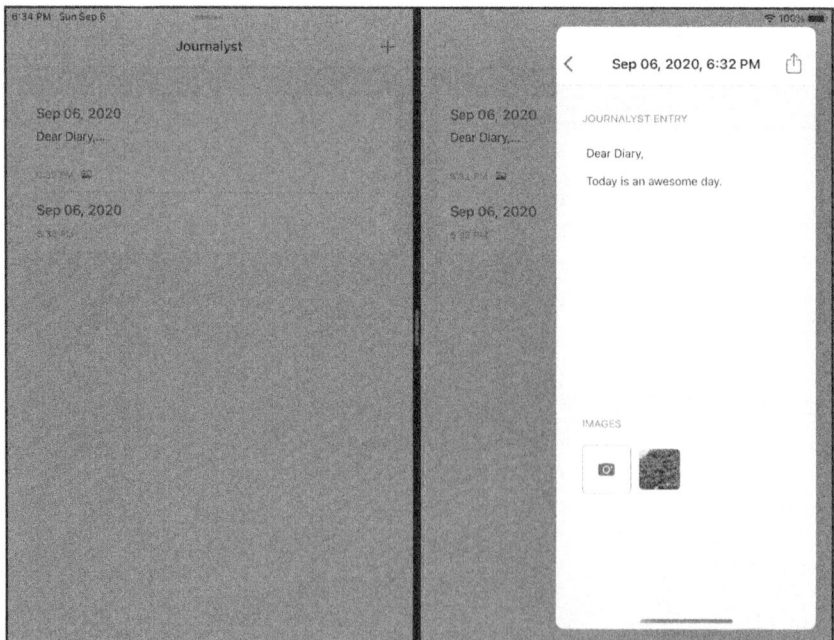

Try it on the Mac

The hard work you put in to make your app support multi-window for iPad has an added bonus: It'll work seamlessly when you run the app on Mac. Open Xcode, select the **My Mac** destination and set your team. Then build and run.

Once the app is running, just press **Command** + **N** and boom!

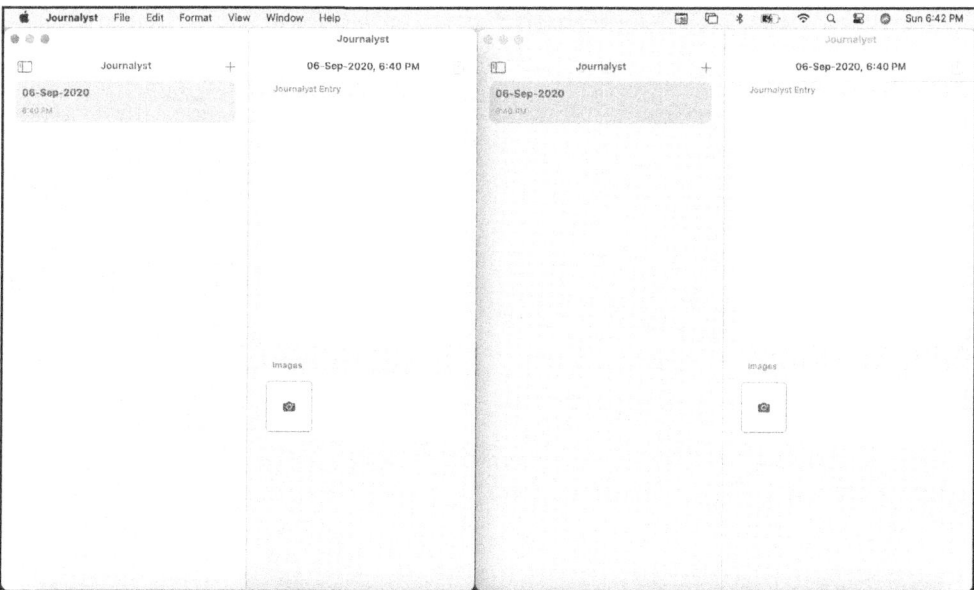

In a later chapter, you'll learn how to add a menu item for spawning a new window, much like you'd find in many Mac apps. But for now, pat yourself on the back and maybe indulge in that tasty dessert you promised yourself earlier.

Key points

- Multi-window is a powerful way to be more productive on iPad and users expect to see it on Mac.

- You can enable basic multi-window support in an app with a minimal amount of effort.

- Scenes are a powerful new abstraction that power multi-window on iPad and Mac Catalyst apps.

- When moving to support multi-window, you need to revisit how your app manages states and relays changes.

- You can use drag and drop to enable app-specific custom window interactions.

In this chapter, you learned what multi-window support is, why you might want to incorporate it into your app, and how to do just that. You also learned about some of the issues that you might introduce when adopting scenes and how to resolve them. Finally, you learned how to go beyond the OS-provided multi-window support by adding a custom window interaction using drag and `NSUserActivity`.

In the next chapter, you'll learn how to add powerful contextual menus to your app so that it's more efficient on iPad and feels even more at home on the Mac.

Chapter 5: Adding Some Context

By Nick Bonatsakis

In the previous chapter, you added multi-window support to your app using scenes.

In this chapter, you'll learn all about context menus, adding support for long press menus on iPad and how those menus will port to Mac automatically.

By the end of this chapter, you'll have learned:

- What contextual menus are and how they can enhance your app's experience.

- How to add basic support for context interactions.

- How to implement basic menu items.

- How to make menu items dynamic.

- How to implement hierarchical menus.

Ready to experience the exciting world of contextual menus? Great! It's time to get started.

Introducing context menus

You might want to jump right in and start coding, but before you get started, you'll need some context around the topic at hand (pun certainly intended). Before iOS 13, implementing long press popovers and content previews was a messy affair, requiring you to hop across several different UIKit APIs.

Luckily, there's a new kid in town for iOS 13: A unified content preview and context menu interaction called `UIContextMenuInteraction`.

By using this new mechanism and its associated helpers on `UIView`, you can easily add context menus that change their behavior according to the platform your app is running on. On iPad, you trigger context menus with a long press gesture. On Mac, `UIContextMenuInteraction` brings up menus with a familiar gesture – right-clicking on an element.

Have a look at this feature in action in the Shortcuts app for iPad. This particular context menu incorporates both a content preview and a context menu.

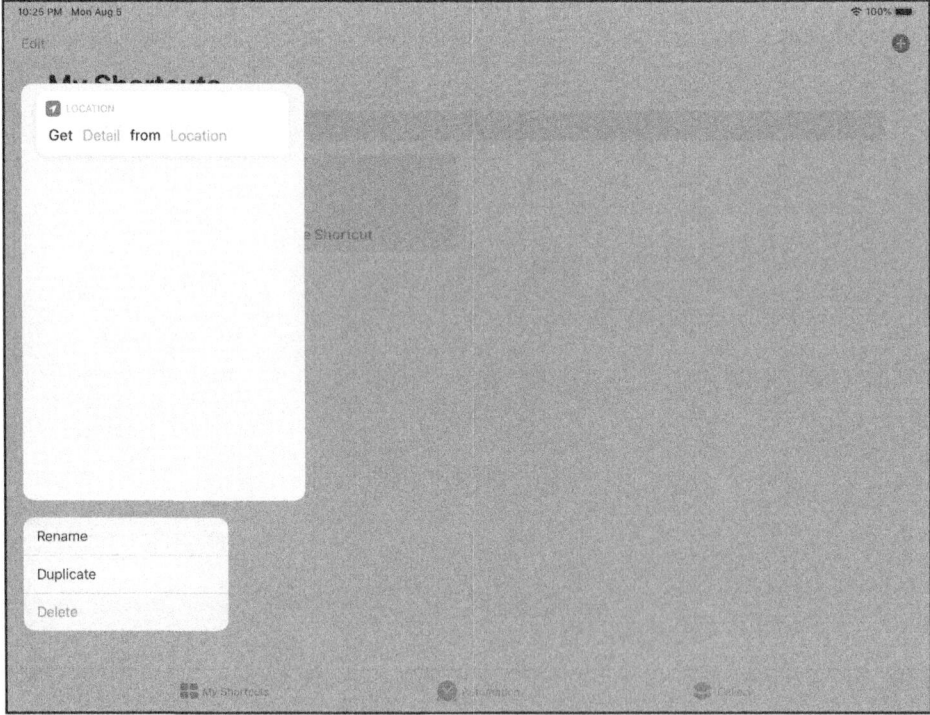

Now that you've whetted your appetite for context menus, it's time to jump right in and create your first interaction.

Adding a context interaction

The most sensible place to enable the Journalyst app's context menus is in the sidebar. Why? Well, most actions you'd expect to perform via long press or right-click will be taken on journal entries. Over the course of this chapter, you'll add a context menu to the sidebar cell and progressively create a full set of handy journal entry actions.

Open the starter project and go to **MainTableViewController.swift**. In `diaryDataSource()`, add the following code right before the `return` statement:

```
let contextInteraction
  = UIContextMenuInteraction(delegate: self)
cell?.addInteraction(contextInteraction)
```

In the above code, you create a new instance of `UIContextMenuInteraction`, passing `self` as the delegate. You'll implement the delegate method in the next step. Then you associate this interaction with the table view cell by calling `addInteraction`, which is a method common to all `UIView` subclasses.

Now, add the following extension to the end of the file:

```
// MARK: UIContextMenuInteractionDelegate
extension MainTableViewController:
  UIContextMenuInteractionDelegate {
  func contextMenuInteraction(
    _ interaction: UIContextMenuInteraction,
    configurationForMenuAtLocation location: CGPoint)
    -> UIContextMenuConfiguration? {
    //1
    let locationInTableView =
      interaction.location(in: tableView)
    //2
    guard let indexPath = tableView
      .indexPathForRow(at: locationInTableView)
      else { return nil }
    //3
    let entry = DataService.shared.allEntries[indexPath.row]
    //4
    return UIContextMenuConfiguration(
      identifier: nil,
      previewProvider: nil) { _ -> UIMenu? in

      //5
      var rootChildren: [UIMenuElement] = []
      //6
      let noOpAction = self.createNoOpAction()
      //7
```

```
        rootChildren.append(noOpAction)
        //8
        let menu = UIMenu(title: "", image: nil,
        identifier: nil, options: [],
        children: rootChildren)
        return menu
      }
    }
  }
```

There's a decent amount of code here, so take a look at it, step-by-step:

1. When the system calls this delegate method, the CGPoint it provides is in the coordinate space of the view that the user interacted with directly – in this case, the UITableViewCell instance. To obtain the index path of the cell, you need the point in terms of the table view's coordinate space, so the first thing you do is obtain that information via the location(in:) method of the interaction instance.

2. Next, armed with the target coordinate in the table view's coordinate space, you attempt to grab the index path for the cell that the user interacted with and bail if it's not found. Returning nil from this method indicates to the system that it shouldn't activate a context menu for the given interaction.

3. Next, you fetch the entry for the given cell by using the index path you obtained above. You'll need the entry object to perform actions on it in the next parts of this chapter.

4. Next, you return an instance of UIContextMenuConfiguration. Passing nil as an identifier will cause the system to generate a unique ID automatically. You also pass nil for previewProvider since you are only going to be adding a menu, not a content preview. The closure here returns the UIMenu instance that implements the menu.

5. Next, you create a mutable array to house the list of top-level menu items. A UIMenu consists of one or more instances of UIMenuElement subclasses.

6. Then, you call a method that returns UIAction.

7. Then, you add the action to the list of root elements.

8. Finally, you create the root UIMenu, passing it an empty title and the root elements list as the children.

Next, add the following method to the same extension:

```
//1
func createNoOpAction() -> UIAction {
  let noOpAction = UIAction(title: "Do Nothing",image: nil,
  identifier: nil, discoverabilityTitle: nil,attributes: [],
  state: .off) { _ in
    // Do nothing
  }
  return noOpAction
}
```

1. Here, you create a method returning `UIAction`, which is a subclass of `UIMenuElement`. This action has a bare-bones configuration with just a title. The trailing block in the initializer is called when the user activates the action (e.g., the user clicks or taps on the menu item). In this case, it does nothing.

Build and run, then long press on a journal entry in the sidebar. You should see the following:

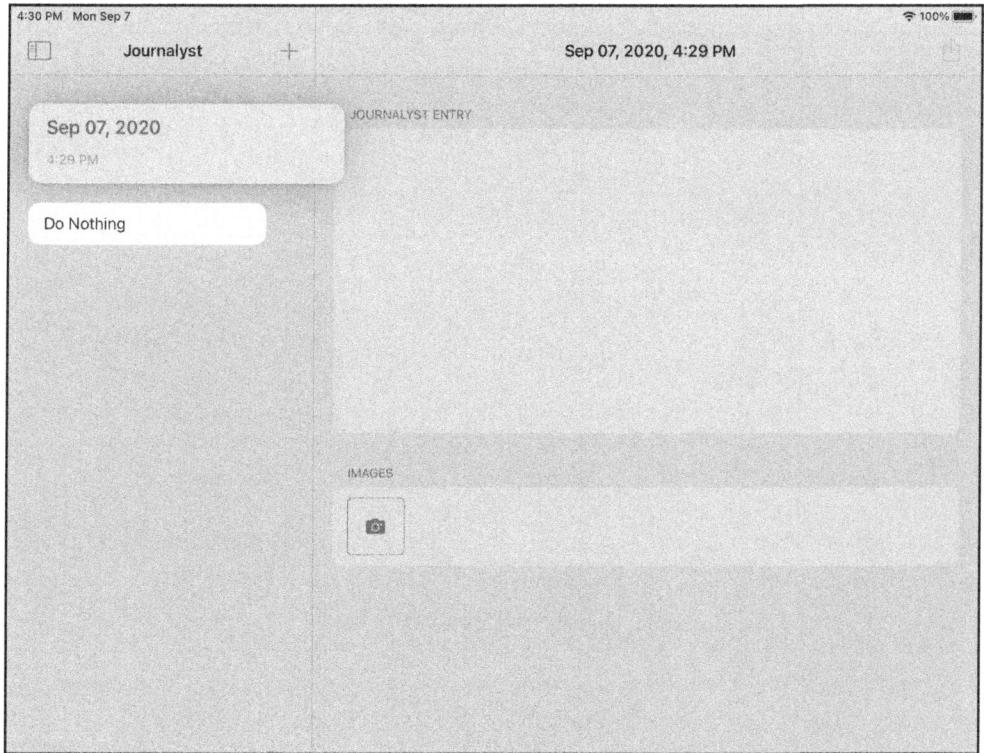

Sweet! Your first context menu. It's not much to look at yet, and it doesn't do anything particularly useful. But you're about to change that…

Opening a new window

In the previous chapter, you learned all about scenes and how they support multi-window configurations in your apps. Recall that you implemented a very nifty custom drag interaction that allows the user to drag a journal entry to create a new window.

An app with great UX often offers the same action via several paths, so that a user is more likely to discover and learn how to perform that action. Context menus are a great place to offer these alternate paths, as users are familiar with long pressing and right-clicking. Wouldn't it be neat to add a menu action for opening an entry in a new window? Why, yes; yes, it would.

First, remove the `createNoOpAction` method that you created. Add a new method as follows:

```
func addOpenNewWindowAction(entry: Entry) -> UIAction {
  //1
  let openInNewWindowAction = UIAction(
    title: "Open in New Window",
    image: UIImage(systemName: "uiwindow.split.2x1"),
    identifier: nil,
    discoverabilityTitle: nil,
    attributes: [],
    state: .off) { _ in
    //2
    self.createNewWindow(for: entry) }
  return openInNewWindowAction
}
```

Back in `contextMenuInteraction` method, remove the code that creates the `noOpAction` and adds it to the `rootChildren` array. Replace it with the following code:

```
let openInNewWindowAction = self.addOpenNewWindowAction(entry:
entry)
//3
rootChildren.append(openInNewWindowAction)
```

The code is similar to the action you added previously, but there are a few things that are different. Here's some more detail about what's going on:

1. As before, you create a new instance of `UIAction`. The most notable difference here is that you pass `UIImage(systemName: "uiwindow.split.2x1")` as the image parameter. This is how you reference an icon from the **SF Symbols** package that Apple introduced in iOS 13.

2. Next, instead of an empty block, you call a method, `createNewWindow(for:)`, that will do the work of creating a new window and passing it the entry.

3. Finally, as before, you add the action to the `rootChildren` array for inclusion in the root menu.

Next, go ahead and implement `createNewWindow(for:)` as follows:

```
func createNewWindow(for entry: Entry) {
  UIApplication.shared.requestSceneSessionActivation(
    nil, userActivity: entry.openDetailUserActivity,
    options: .none, errorHandler: nil)
}
```

Just one line of code is all it takes to get this one done. You call `requestSceneSessionActivation(_:userActivity:options:errorHandler:)` on the shared `UIApplication`, passing it `entry.openDetailUserActivity` to preconfigure the new window to display the provided entry.

Build and run to see the fruits of your labor. Try tapping on **Open in New Window** to see this action work in all its glory.

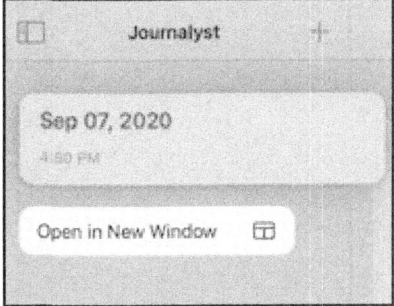

Creating a new entry

Oftentimes, apps that manage lists of data include a menu action that lets its users create a new instance of a given entity. Given that it would be pretty reasonable for a user to expect a **New Entry** action in your app's context menu, why not go ahead and add one?

Start by adding the following method:

```
func addNewEntryAction(entry: Entry) -> UIAction {
  let newEntryAction = UIAction(
    title: "New Entry",
```

```
      image: UIImage(systemName: "square.and.pencil"),
      identifier: nil,
      discoverabilityTitle: nil,
      attributes: [],
      state: .off) { _ in
      self.createEntry()
  }
  return newEntryAction
}
```

Add the following code to `contextMenuInteraction`, after you append `openInNewWindowAction`:

```
let newEntryAction = self.addNewEntryAction(entry: entry)
rootChildren.append(newEntryAction)
```

This code is similar to the code you used to add the **Open in New Window** action. It configures the action, implements a handler, calls a method, `createEntry()`, to do the work of creating the new entry, then finally adds the action to the list of root menu children.

To finish up, implement `createEntry()` as follows:

```
func createEntry() {
   DataService.shared.addEntry(Entry())
}
```

Nothing too crazy here, just another one-liner, this time creating a new entry via the `DataService` class. Since the data flow is tied together using `NotificationCenter`, that's all you need to do to make a new entry and have it show up in the UI.

Build and run once more, then check out the context menu again. You should now be able to create new entries in a snap.

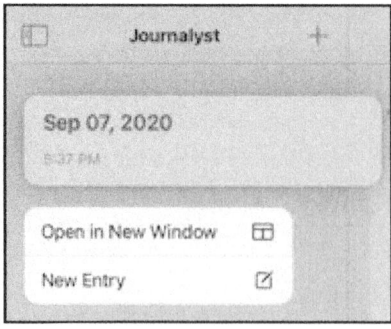

Adding an image to an entry

Another action that would be pretty useful to have in the context menu for journal entries is the ability to directly add images. Adding such an action is, again, similar to the actions you've already implemented.

Start by once again adding the following method.

```
func addImageAction(entry: Entry, indexPath: IndexPath) ->
UIAction {
  let addImageAction = UIAction(
    title: "Add Image",
    image: UIImage(systemName: "photo"),
    identifier: nil,
    discoverabilityTitle: nil,
    attributes: [],
    state: .off) { _ in
    self.addImage(to: entry, indexPath: indexPath)
  }
  return addImageAction
}
```

Then, add the following code to `contextMenuInteraction`, after you append `newEntryAction`:

```
let addImageAction = self.addImageAction(entry: entry,
indexPath: indexPath)
rootChildren.append(addImageAction)
```

Again, there's nothing new here compared with the previous few actions, so jump right into implementing `addImage(to:indexPath:)` as follows:

```
func addImage(to entry: Entry, indexPath: IndexPath) {
  //1
  let cell = tableView.cellForRow(at: indexPath)
  //2
  photoPicker.present(in: self,
    sourceView: cell) {image, _ in
    //3
    if let image = image {
      var newEntry = entry
      newEntry.images.append(image)
      DataService.shared.updateEntry(newEntry)
    }
  }
}
```

The above code is a bit more involved than the previous few action handlers, so reviewing it in detail:

1. You obtain a reference to the `UITableViewCell` that activated the interaction.

2. Next, you call `present` on `PhotoPicker` to launch an action sheet that allows the user to select an image from either their library or the camera, if it's available. You pass `UITableViewCell` here so that when the app runs on iPad and Mac, the action sheet is anchored to that element.

3. Finally, if the user selects an image, you handle it by creating a mutable copy of the entry, adding the image to it and then persisting the change to the data service.

Build and run, then activate the menu again and you'll find that you can now add images to a journal entry directly from the sidebar.

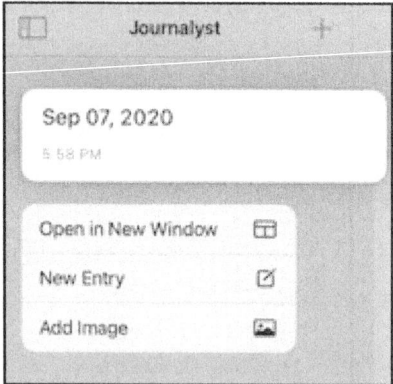

Add an entry to favorites

The next menu action you'll implement allows a user to add and remove a journal entry as a favorite. At present, there isn't a way to filter by favorite entries. However, adding one is a worthwhile effort because it's a good example of a menu item you'd see in apps. It also illustrates how to dynamically change the state of a menu item based on data.

Before you add the menu item, you'll need to tweak the journal entry model and the UI associated with it to support favorites. First, open **Entry.swift** and add the following property to the struct:

```
var isFavorite = false
```

Then change the implementation of == to incorporate the new property as follows:

```
static func == (lhs: Entry, rhs: Entry) -> Bool {
  return lhs.dateCreated == rhs.dateCreated &&
    lhs.log ?? "" == rhs.log ?? "" &&
    lhs.images == rhs.images &&
    lhs.isFavorite == rhs.isFavorite
}
```

Finally, you'll want to add a visual indicator to the entry cells so your users can see at a glance if an entry is a favorite. Open **EntryTableViewCell.swift** and add the following code to the didSet block on entry:

```
accessoryView = entry.isFavorite
  ? UIImageView(image: UIImage(systemName: "star.fill"))
  : nil
```

The above code sets the cell's accessory view to an SF Symbols star icon if the entry is a favorite; otherwise, it's set to nil.

You're now ready to add the new menu action. Jump back to **MainTableViewController.swift** and add the following method to UIContextMenuInteractionDelegate extension.

```
func addFavoriteAction(entry: Entry) -> UIAction {
  //1
  let favoriteTitle = entry.isFavorite ? "Remove from Favorites"
: "Add to Favorites"
  //2
  let favoriteImageName = entry.isFavorite ? "star.slash" :
"star"
  //3
  let favoriteAction = UIAction(
    title: favoriteTitle,
    image: UIImage(systemName: favoriteImageName),
    identifier: nil,
    discoverabilityTitle: nil,
    attributes: [],
    state: .off) { _ in self.toggleFavorite(for: entry)
  }
  return favoriteAction
}
```

Then, add the following code to contextMenuInteraction, after you append addImageAction:

```
let favoriteAction = self.addFavoriteAction(entry: entry)
//4
rootChildren.append(favoriteAction)
```

Here's what this code is doing:

1. First, you create a title variable that prompts the user to "Add to Favorites" if the entry is not a favorite, or "Remove from Favorites" if it already is.

2. You create a variable to represent the icon you want to use: A star if the action is "Add to Favorites" or a star with a slash through it for the "Remove from Favorites" action.

3. Now, you create the menu action, passing it the variables you defined and calling `toggleFavorite` in the handler.

4. Finally, as always, you add the action to the root children array for inclusion in the menu.

To finish up this action, implement `toggleFavorite` like so:

```
func toggleFavorite(for entry: Entry) {
  var newEntry = entry
  newEntry.isFavorite.toggle()
  DataService.shared.updateEntry(newEntry)
}
```

In the above code, you make a mutable copy of the provided entry, toggle the `isFavorite` property and persist the change to the data service.

Build and run, then bring up the context menu again. Try toggling the favorite state of an entry and you should see both the entry cell and the menu option change.

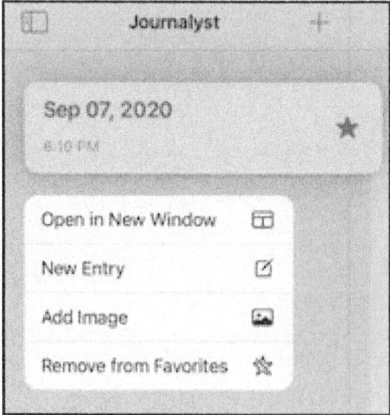

Sharing an entry

Your journal entry context menu is really starting to take shape now, but you're not done yet. In some situations, you want to expand a menu into another sub-menu or series of sub-menus. Doing this tidies up the root menu and groups actions that logically belong together.

To learn how to add one of these nested menus, you're going to add a "Share" menu item that triggers a sub-menu with several share options.

Still inside **MainTableViewController.swift**, add the following method to `UIContextMenuInteractionDelegate` extension:

```swift
func addShareMenu(entry: Entry, indexPath: IndexPath) -> UIMenu
{
  //1
  let copyAction = UIAction(
    title: "Copy",
    image: UIImage(systemName: "doc.on.doc"),
    identifier: nil,
    discoverabilityTitle: nil,
    attributes: [],
    state: .off) { _ in self.copy(contentsOf: entry) }
  //2
  let moreAction = UIAction(
    title: "More",
    image: UIImage(systemName: "ellipsis"),
    identifier: nil,
    discoverabilityTitle: nil,
    attributes: [],
    state: .off) { _ in self.share(entry, at: indexPath) }
  //3
  let shareMenu = UIMenu(
    title: "Share",
    image: UIImage(systemName: "square.and.arrow.up"),
    identifier: nil,
    options: [],
    children: [copyAction, moreAction])
  return shareMenu
}
```

Then, add the following code to `contextMenuInteraction`, after you append `favoriteAction`:

```swift
let shareMenu = self.addShareMenu(entry: entry, indexPath:
indexPath)
//4
rootChildren.append(shareMenu)
```

This code looks similar to the code for creating a regular menu action. Here's a detailed breakdown of what it does:

1. First, you create a menu action to copy the contents of an entry. This is the first menu item for the sub-menu.

2. Next, you create the second sub-menu action, a menu item that brings up the system share sheet for more options.

3. You then create the share menu for inclusion in the root menu, passing the two sub-menu actions as children.

4. Finally, you add the share menu to the root children array so that it gets included in the root menu.

Next, implement the two methods that do the work for the share sub-menu actions like this:

```swift
func copy(contentsOf entry: Entry) {
  if entry.log != nil {
    //1
    UIPasteboard.general.string = entry.log
  }
}

func share(_ entry: Entry, at indexPath: IndexPath) {
  //2
  var items: [Any] = []
  if let log = entry.log {
    items.append(log)
  }
  if !entry.images.isEmpty {
    items.append(contentsOf: entry.images)
  }
  //3
  let activityController = UIActivityViewController(
    activityItems: items,
    applicationActivities: nil)
    //4
    if let popoverController =
      activityController.popoverPresentationController,
      let cell = tableView.cellForRow(at: indexPath) {
        popoverController.sourceView = cell
        popoverController.sourceRect = cell.bounds
        //5
        present(activityController, animated: true,
                completion: nil)
  }
}
```

Taking the above code, step by step:

1. First, you implement `copy(contentsOf:)` by setting the system paste board's string to the journal entry text.

2. You implement `share(_:at:)` by first declaring an array for the activity items and then populating the array with the entry text and images.

3. Now, you create a new instance of `UIActivityViewController` with the activity items.

4. You then configure the activity view controller's presentation to anchor on the relevant cell if it's running on larger-screen platforms.

5. Finally, you present the share sheet activity as you would any other view controller.

Build and run yet again and you'll find a new "Share" menu item that should, when tapped on, bring up the sub-menu you see below.

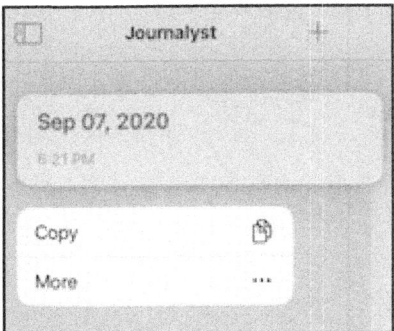

Deleting an entry

There's just one more action to go before you have a fully-armed and operational context menu. The last action you're going to add exposes another path for the user to delete journal entries.

Continuing in **MainTableViewController.swift**, add the following code to `UIContextMenuInteractionDelegate` extension:

```swift
func addDeleteAction(indexPath: IndexPath) -> UIAction {
  let deleteAction = UIAction(
    title: "Delete",
    image: UIImage(systemName: "trash"),
```

```
      identifier: nil,
      discoverabilityTitle: nil,
      attributes: .destructive,
      state: .off) { _ in self.removeEntry(at: indexPath) }
    return deleteAction
  }
```

Then, add the following code to `contextMenuInteraction`, after you append `shareMenu`:

```
let deleteAction = self.addDeleteAction(indexPath: indexPath)
rootChildren.append(deleteAction)
```

This code's almost identical to all the other menu actions you've implemented, but there's one difference worth noting: You pass `.destructive` as an attribute. This will give the menu title and icon a red color and clearly indicate to the user that this action is destructive and potentially dangerous.

Now, add the following method to delete the entry when the user activates this menu action:

```
func removeEntry(at indexPath: IndexPath) {
  DataService.shared.removeEntry(atIndex: indexPath.row)
}
```

There's nothing complicated about the above code, it just removes the entry via the data service. Once again, data changes will propagate to the UI via notifications, so this is all that's needed to implement this action.

Build and run one last time and you'll see the finished menu, complete with the ability to delete an entry.

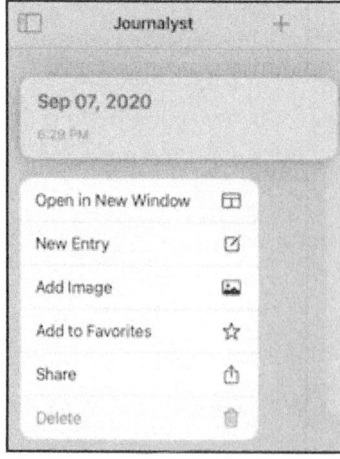

Try it on macOS

Now that you've gone to the trouble of implementing context menus for iPad, you'll find that you get the same support for free when running on Mac.

On the Mac, the menus' look and feel automatically adjust to align with standard Mac menus. Your users will have a familiar experience.

Switch your run location to **My Mac** and build and run. Right-click on a journal entry in the sidebar and explore the various actions and sub-menus.

Key points

- Context menus are a powerful way to expose alternate paths for common app actions.

- iOS offers a unified mechanism for creating context menus that work on iPad and Mac.

- Context menus can be as simple as singular actions or as complex as multi-level hierarchical menus.

Chapter 6: The Keyboard

By Andy Pereira

The physical keyboard is something that has always been part of the personal computer experience. But, when iOS was introduced, it *almost* seemed like the idea of a software keyboard would take over. Luckily, for those that like a real keyboard, Apple introduced support not only for physical keyboards on iOS but keyboard shortcuts.

While keyboards shortcuts might go overlooked on iOS apps, macOS users expect them. In this chapter, you'll learn how to add shortcuts, what modifier keys are, and how to combine them with key combinations to quickly perform tasks in your app.

Getting started

Open the starter project for the chapter. It will be best if you can run this app on a physical iOS or iPadOS device, with a physical keyboard paired with the device. Using the simulator will work, but you may notice some performance issues.

First responders

Before you add the shortcuts, it will help to understand a little bit about the responder chain and the first responder. `UIViewControllers`, `UIViews` and `UIApplication` are all classes that can receive and handle events, otherwise known as responder objects. Since you can add keyboard shortcuts to any of these kinds of classes, you'll need to tell the system which responder is the class in the responder chain that will receive the keyboard event first. This is referred to as the first responder.

To start, open **RootSplitViewController.swift** and add the following:

```
// MARK: - Keyboard Commands
override var canBecomeFirstResponder: Bool {
  true
}
```

Now, when you perform a keyboard shortcut, `RootSplitViewController` will be able to receive and respond to it.

Adding the commands

Keyboard shortcuts can be performed by simply pressing a single key on the keyboard or multiple keys. They can also be used in conjunction with modifiers keys, like Command, Control and Option. You're going to add three shortcuts that each use modifier keys.

Open **RootSplitViewController.swift** and add the following methods:

```
@objc private func addEntry(sender: UIKeyCommand) {
}

@objc private func goToPrevious(sender: UIKeyCommand) {
}
```

```
@objc private func goToNext(sender: UIKeyCommand) {
}
```

For now, these don't do anything. You need them because keyboard shortcuts need actions to call. You'll come back to this later in the chapter.

Now you can start adding key commands. Add the following in **RootSplitViewController.swift**:

```
override var keyCommands: [UIKeyCommand]? {
  let newKeyCommand
    = UIKeyCommand(input: "N",
                   modifierFlags: .control,
                   action: #selector(addEntry(sender:)))
  newKeyCommand.discoverabilityTitle = "Add Entry"
  return [newKeyCommand]
}
```

Here, you've added a key command for adding a new entry. It's important to know what is happening:

- `input`: This is the actual key that will trigger the action to be called.

- `modifierFlags`: In this example, you've added `.control`, which means your shortcut will be performed by pressing Control-N.

- `action`: This is the method called when the shortcut is performed.

- `discoverabilityTitle`: When you have a physical keyboard attached to your iOS device, holding Command down will show the Discoverability window or layer. It lists all the keyboard shortcuts available in the current application. Adding the `discoverabilityTitle` is required to list the shortcut in the Discoverability window.

Overriding `keyCommands` is how you inform the responder chain what key commands the current responder supports. It is important to note that the system reserves certain key commands for itself, which you cannot override. For example, Cut, Copy and Paste's key combinations cannot be changed for yourself. Because Command-N is reserved for opening a new window, you use the modifier to make Control-N create the entry.

Build and run, and hold down **Command** to make the Discoverability window appear.

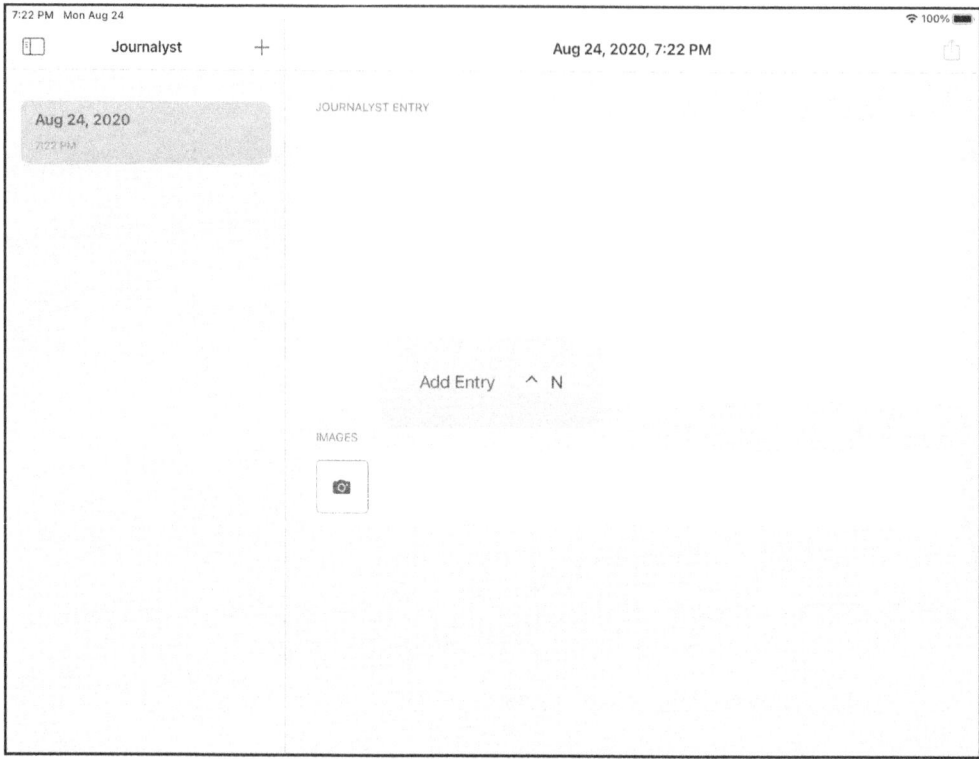

If you are having trouble with keyboard shortcuts within the simulator, you may need to use the **Capture Keyboard** functionality. You can select this in the toolbar of your iPad simulator, as shown below:

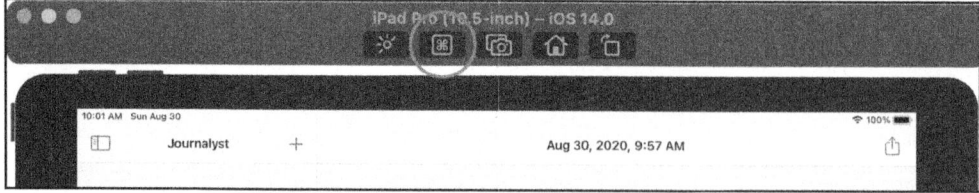

To exit keyboard capture mode, you can select the button again, or press **Escape**.

To get the application to add an entry when using the key combination, add this line to addEntry:

```
DataService.shared.addEntry(Entry())
```

Build and run, and then press **Control-N**. You should now see a new entry show up in the list.

To get the remaining key commands set up, replace keyCommands with the following:

```
override var keyCommands: [UIKeyCommand]? {
  let newKeyCommand
    = UIKeyCommand(input: "N",
                   modifierFlags: .control,
                   action: #selector(addEntry(sender:)))
  newKeyCommand.discoverabilityTitle = "Add Entry"
  let upKeyCommand
    = UIKeyCommand(input: "[",
                   modifierFlags: [.command, .shift],
                   action: #selector(goToPrevious(sender:)))
  upKeyCommand.discoverabilityTitle = "Previous Entry"
  let downKeyCommand
    = UIKeyCommand(input: "]",
                   modifierFlags: [.command, .shift],
                   action: #selector(goToNext(sender:)))
  downKeyCommand.discoverabilityTitle = "Next Entry"
  return [newKeyCommand, upKeyCommand, downKeyCommand]
}
```

The final two key commands will allow the user to select the previous or next entry in the entry list. While almost the same as newKeyCommand, these take multiple modifier keys to perform. It requires Command-Shift-[to be pressed to go back in the list, and Command-Shift-] to move forward.

While you can decide which modifiers are used, remember to keep the combinations simple enough for your user to remember.

Build and run, and hold down **Command** to show the Discoverability window. You should now see all three of your keyboard shortcuts:

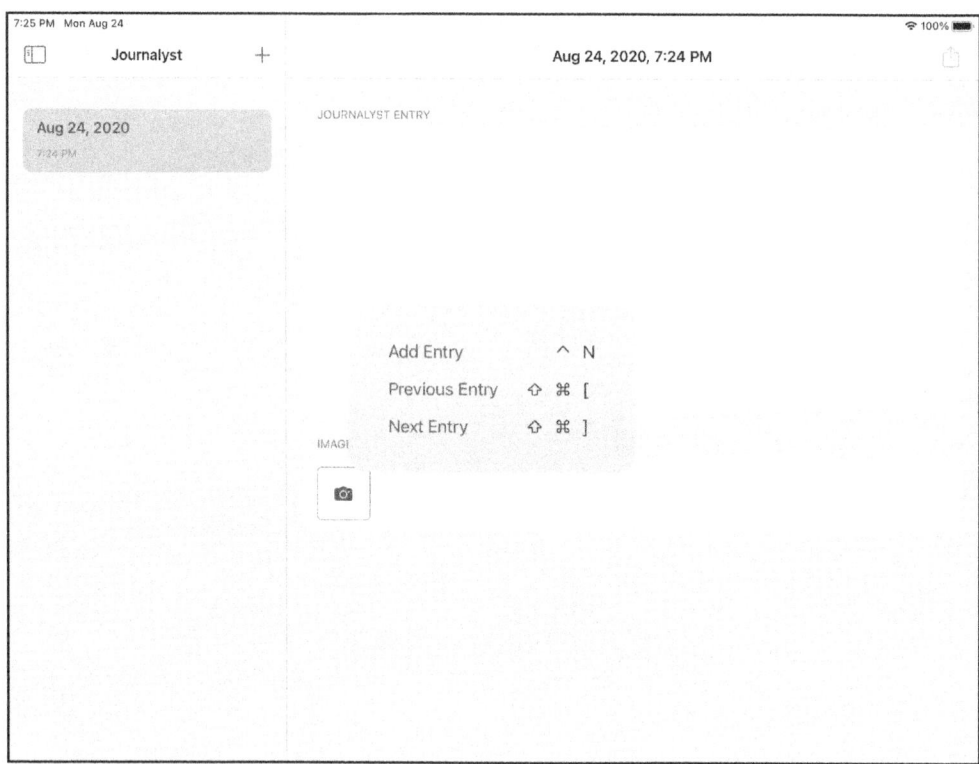

Now, your last step is to actually do something when the keys are pressed. Open **RootSplitViewController.swift** and add this code to `goToPrevious`:

```
guard let navigationController =
  viewControllers.first as? UINavigationController,
  let mainTableViewController =
  navigationController.topViewController
    as? MainTableViewController else { return }
mainTableViewController.goToPrevious()
```

And add this code to `goToNext`:

```
guard let navigationController =
  viewControllers.first as? UINavigationController,
  let mainTableViewController =
  navigationController.topViewController
    as? MainTableViewController else { return }
mainTableViewController.goToNext()
```

Now, open **MainTableViewController.swift**, and add the following methods:

```swift
func goToPrevious() {
  guard let index = indexOfCurrentEntry(),
    index > 0 else { return }
  let previousIndex = index - 1
  let indexPath = IndexPath(row: previousIndex,
                            section: 0)
  tableView.selectRow(at: indexPath,
                      animated: false,
                      scrollPosition: .middle)
  performSegue(withIdentifier: "ShowEntrySegue",
               sender: tableView.cellForRow(at: indexPath))
}

func goToNext() {
  guard let index = indexOfCurrentEntry(),
    index < DataService.shared.allEntries.count - 1 else
{ return }
  let nextIndex = index + 1
  let indexPath = IndexPath(row: nextIndex,
                            section: 0)
  tableView.selectRow(at: indexPath,
                      animated: false,
                      scrollPosition: .middle)
  performSegue(withIdentifier: "ShowEntrySegue",
               sender: tableView.cellForRow(at: indexPath))
}
```

When performing the "Previous Entry" and "Next Entry" shortcuts, these methods will handle going to the previous and next entries.

Build and run, and try using the keyboard shortcuts. Press **Control-N** to add a few entries, and **Command-Shift-[** and **Command-Shift-]** to move through the list.

Last, add the final keyboard shortcut to delete an entry. In **RootSplitViewController.swift**, add the following to the end of keyCommands *replacing* the existing return line:

```swift
let deleteKeyCommand
  = UIKeyCommand(input: "\u{8}",
                modifierFlags: [.command],
                action: #selector(removeEntry(sender:)))
deleteKeyCommand.discoverabilityTitle = "Delete Entry"

return [newKeyCommand, upKeyCommand,
  downKeyCommand, deleteKeyCommand]
```

This will add the shortcut to delete an entry when pressing **Command-Delete**. To display the macOS system symbol for Delete, and respond to it being pressed, you use the Unicode symbol for BACKSPACE, which is **8**.

Then, add the following method in the same file:

```
@objc private func removeEntry(sender: UIKeyCommand) {
  guard let navigationController = viewControllers.first
    as? UINavigationController,
    let mainTableViewController
      = navigationController.topViewController
      as? MainTableViewController else { return }
  mainTableViewController.deleteCurrentEntry()
}
```

Finally, add the following method to **MainTableViewController.swift**:

```
func deleteCurrentEntry() {
  guard let index = indexOfCurrentEntry() else { return }
  DataService.shared.removeEntry(atIndex: index)
  var indexPath = IndexPath(row: index,
                            section: 0)
  guard tableView.numberOfRows(inSection: 0) > 0 else {
    performSegue(withIdentifier: "ShowEntrySegue", sender: nil)
    return
  }
  if index == tableView.numberOfRows(inSection: 0) {
    indexPath = IndexPath(row: index - 1,
                          section: 0)
  }
  tableView.selectRow(at: indexPath,
                      animated: false,
                      scrollPosition: .middle)
  performSegue(withIdentifier: "ShowEntrySegue",
               sender: tableView.cellForRow(at: indexPath))
}
```

The last thing you've added here supports responding to the keyboard shortcut and deleting the entry that is selected in the table view.

The examples in this chapter used an input that directly relates to what you see on the keyboard or its Unicode symbol. However, there are constants defined for a few keys which you'll need to use if you want to respond to Escape or any of the directional arrows:

- UIKeyCommand.`inputUpArrow`
- UIKeyCommand.`inputDownArrow`
- UIKeyCommand.`inputLeftArrow`
- UIKeyCommand.`inputRightArrow`
- UIKeyCommand.`inputEscape`

Alternate keyboard handling

The previous section handled adding keyboard shortcuts in a way that enabled discoverability for the user. However, you may not want to inundate your users with all the key commands you would like to support, especially if there are multiple options available.

Open **MainTableViewController.swift**, and add the following methods to the main class body:

```
override var canBecomeFirstResponder: Bool { true }

override func pressesBegan(_ presses: Set<UIPress>,
                           with event: UIPressesEvent?) {
  for press in presses {
    guard let key = press.key else { continue }
    switch key.keyCode {
    case .keyboardUpArrow,
         .keyboardLeftArrow: goToPrevious()
    case .keyboardDownArrow,
         .keyboardRightArrow: goToNext()
    default:
      super.pressesBegan(presses, with: event)
    }
  }
}
```

This is an older way to handle keyboard input. Here, you're simply listening for when keyboard presses begin and respond to the desired keyCodes. In this example, you've added the ability to use the up, down, left and right keys to cycle through entries in the sidebar.

Key Points

- Providing keyboard shortcuts is essential for macOS users, and is becoming more expected for iPadOS users.

- UIKeyCommand makes setting up keyboard shortcuts easy, and works across iOS and macOS.

- Ensure you handle typical shortcuts for keys that aren't automatically supported by the operating system.

Where to go from here?

Your app is now set to handle shortcuts. While Catalyst will automatically handle these keyboard shortcuts, you'll learn later on how to make sure these shortcuts are shown in the Menu bar.

You can learn more about UIKeyCommand on Apple's website: https://developer.apple.com/documentation/uikit/uikeycommand

There's more you can learn about the responder chain, as well, from Apple's website: https://developer.apple.com/documentation/appkit/nsresponder

Chapter 7: Preferences & Settings Bundle

By Andy Pereira

Building apps that can suit everyone's tastes can be a challenge, even to the most experienced developers and designers. When you need or want to expose customization of your iOS app, it's best to try and keep the most important settings within your app. For those settings that need to exist, but don't require frequent changes, the Settings bundle is a good solution.

The **Human Interface Guidelines** (https://apple.co/2HY5vtf) caution against putting frequently used settings within the iOS Settings app. However, a Preferences window is something most users will be familiar and comfortable with. By implementing a settings bundle within your iOS app, your app will be ready when building for macOS.

Getting started

To begin, open the starter project for this chapter. Select any iPad for the active scheme, then build and run. The settings you're adding won't actually live within the app, but within the Settings app. Press the **Home** button on the simulator, and open **Settings**. Right now, you'll see only the default settings.

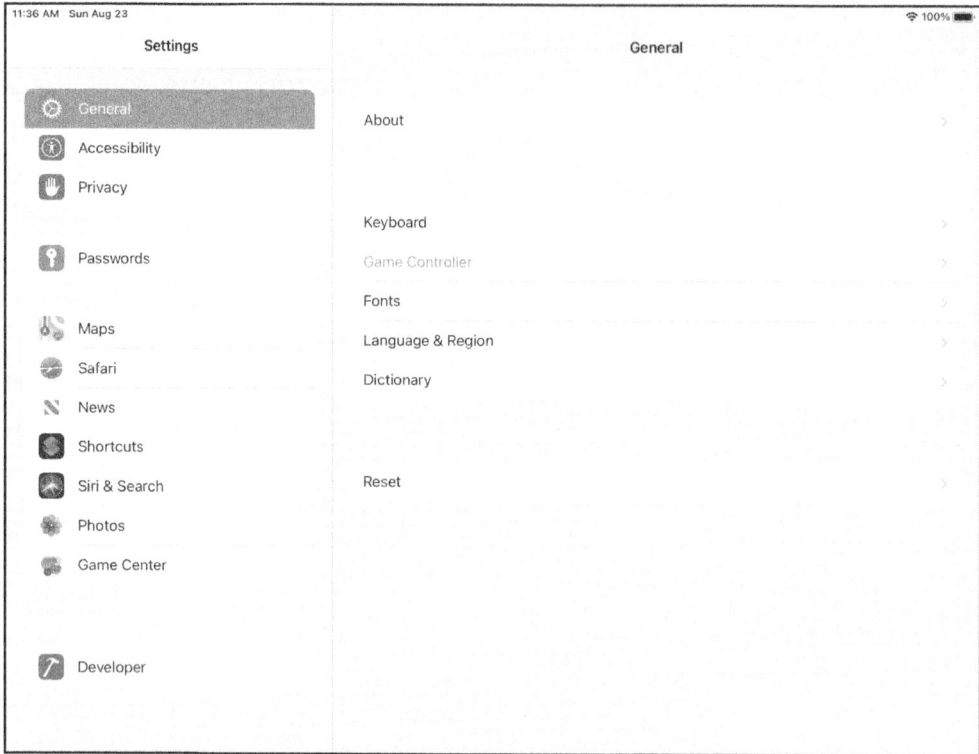

You're going to add a few preferences to this app:

- Currently, when the app runs with the system in dark mode, it will make the text view dark. Sometimes, users might prefer the area they type or read to be lighter. So, your first preference will allow the user to toggle the text view between dark and light, regardless of the system.

- Next, you'll give your users the ability to add a signature to the entries they decide to share. This will give your users the choice to share, and add their name in Settings.

Adding the settings bundle

To add your app and its settings to the system Settings app, in your project, select the **Journalyst** group, and then **File ▸ New ▸ File…**. Under the Resource header, select **Settings Bundle**.

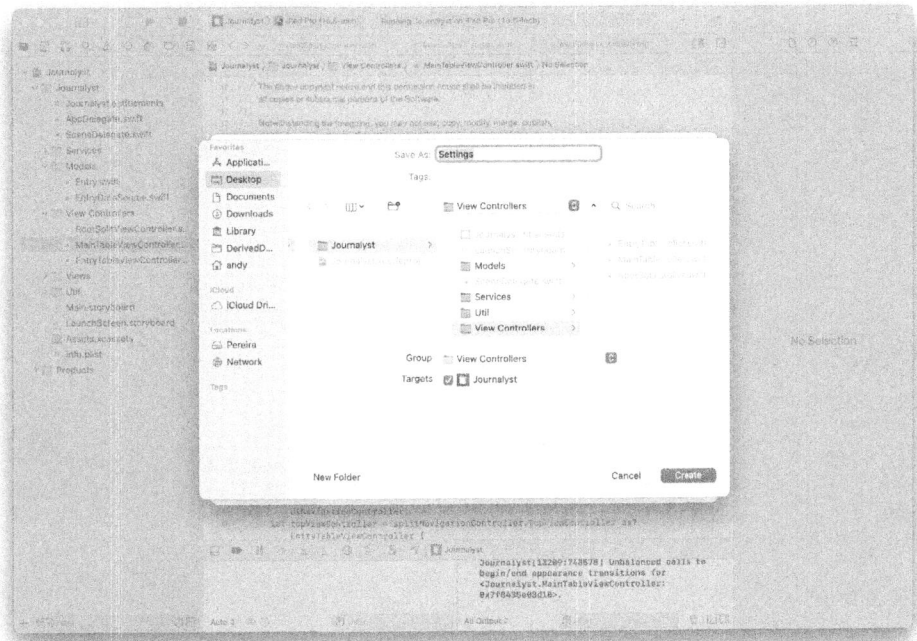

Select **Next** then **Create**. You will now have Settings.bundle in your app's files. There are two files that are created by default for you:

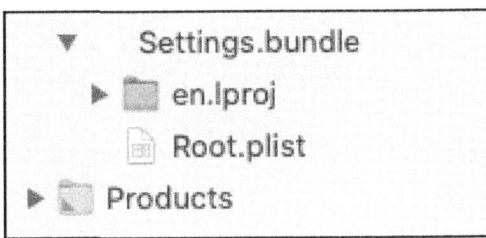

1. **Root.strings**: If you want to localize the strings in your settings, the localizations will need to live here. You don't have any access to your app's code within **Settings**, so this allows you to still support any translations your app does.

2. **Root.plist**: This is where your settings will live.

Build and run, and switch back to **Settings**. You'll now see your app is available, with some default preferences.

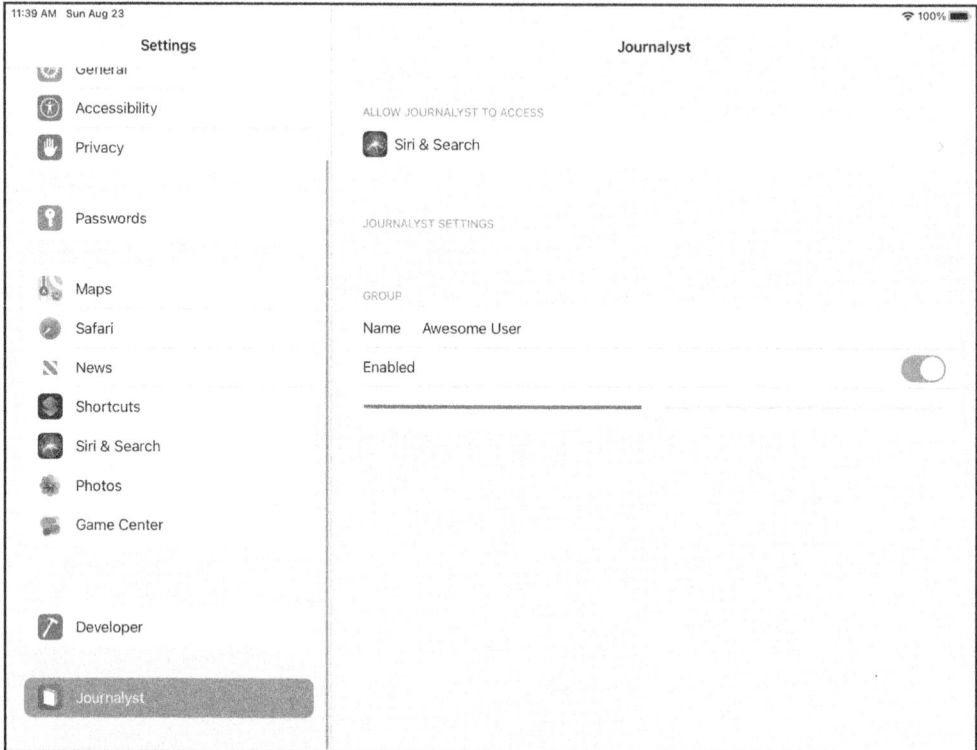

Back in Xcode, open **Root.plist**. Then, expand the entries so you can see all of the items under **Preference Items**. Each one corresponds to what you saw in Settings. Delete each item under Preference Items by highlighting one item at a time and selecting **Edit ▸ Delete**.

> **Note**: The plist editor won't let you select multiple items at a time.

Select **Preference Items**, and then from the menu, select **Editor ▸ Add Item**. Repeat this two more times, reselecting Preference Items each time. Because the plist editor can be finicky when attempting to rearrange items, it'll be easier to add all three right now. Expand **Item 0**, and use the toggle arrows at the far right for **Type** and change it to **Toggle Switch**:

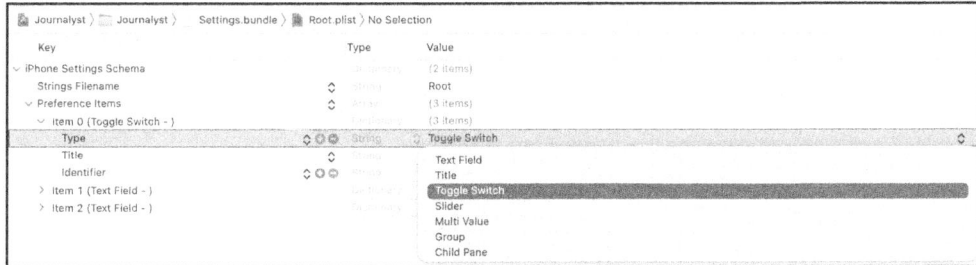

Set the other values to the following:

- **Title**: Include Signature When Sharing

- **Identifier**: signature_preference

Although you've added a "toggle switch" in the context of settings, the user will see a familiar **UISwitch**. The title you entered will be displayed to the left of the toggle.

In both iOS and macOS, your app's preferences or settings can be a property stored within the user defaults. Whenever the toggle value is changed, it will use Identifier to know what key to save the value to in the user defaults.

With Item 0 highlighted, select **Editor ▸ Add Item**. Set the newly added key and value to the following:

- **Key**: Default Value

- **Value**: NO

This will give your user default an initial value, allowing the system to know what to set the toggle to initially.

Next, set the following values for **Item 1** in **Preferences Items**:

- **Type**: Text Field

- **Title**: Name When Sharing

- **Identifier**: name_preference

- **Keyboard Type**: Alphabet

- **Autocapitalization Style**: Words

- **Autocorrection Style**: No Autocorrection

This will add a text field that the user can enter their name in.

And finally add the following items for **Item 2**:

- **Type**: Toggle Switch

- **Title**: Show Entry With Light Background

- **Identifier**: entry_color_preference

- **Default Value**: NO

This setting will allow the user to decide whether or not they want the text view to always be a light color, regardless of whether the system is in dark mode or not.

Build and run, go to **Settings**, and you'll now see all of your new items.

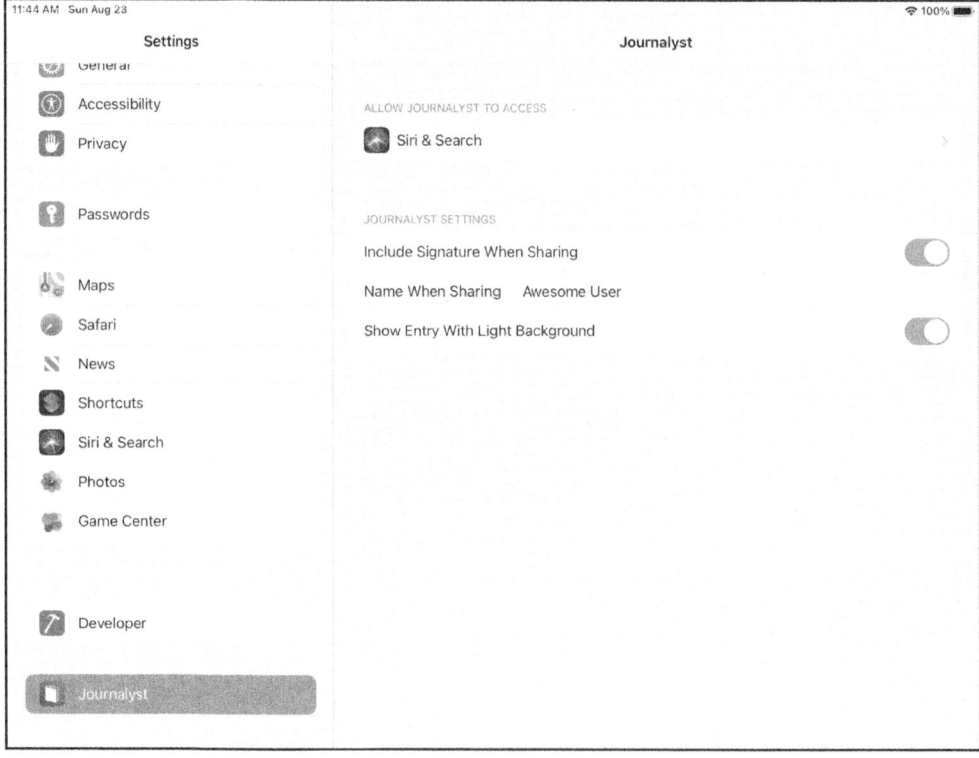

Responding to change

You won't be able to actually see any changes if you don't listen for changes to user defaults. Open **EntryTableViewController.swift**, and add the following to the end of `viewDidLoad()`:

```
UserDefaults.standard
.addObserver(self,
            forKeyPath: colorPreference,
            options: .new,
            context: nil)
```

Apple states that changes to a setting should have an immediate effect on the app, so you want to observe when the user defaults change. Here, you've set your view controller to observe when user defaults changes the key `entry_color_preference`.

Next, add the following methods to **EntryTableViewController**:

```
override func observeValue(forKeyPath keyPath: String?,
                           of object: Any?,
                           change: [NSKeyValueChangeKey : Any]?,
                           context: UnsafeMutableRawPointer?) {
  if keyPath == colorPreference {
    updateEntryCellColor()
  }
}

private func updateEntryCellColor() {
  let overrideColorPreference = UserDefaults
    .standard.bool(forKey: colorPreference)
  if overrideColorPreference {
    entryCell.contentView.backgroundColor = .white
    textView.textColor = .black
  } else {
    entryCell.contentView.backgroundColor = nil
    textView.textColor = .label
  }
}
```

The first method you added will be called when a user changes the toggle for **Show Entry With Light Background**.

The second method checks if the toggle value is true. If so, it overrides the text color of the text view to be black, and the background color of the cell to be white. If the value is false, it will use the default label and cell background colors.

Build and run. Then still in Xcode, use Environment Overrides (**Debug ▸ View Debugging ▸ Configure Environment Overrides**) to change Interface Style to **Dark**.

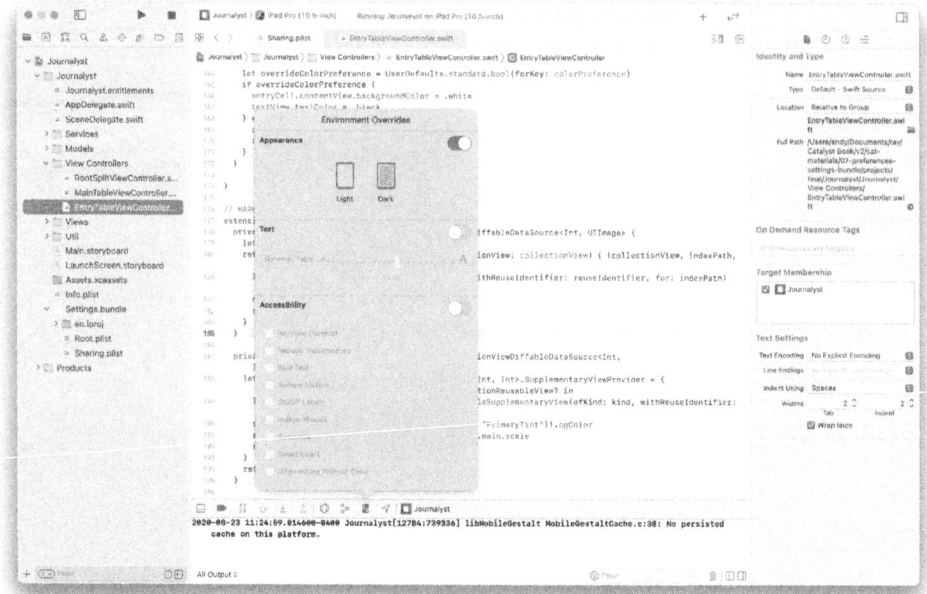

Now on the iPad, you can go back to **Settings** and set the toggle for **Show Entry With Light Background** to true. When you return to the app, your text area should appear white. Try changing the interface style toggle back and forth to see how it changes properly.

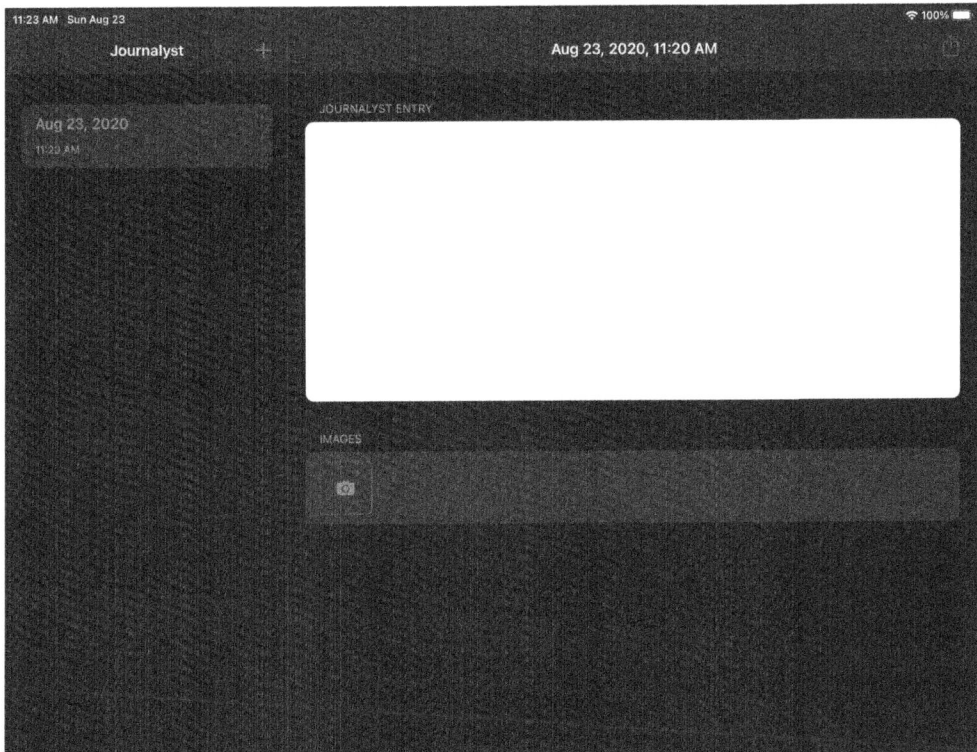

Next, back in Xcode, and the following property to **EntryTableViewController.swift**:

```
private var shareText: String? {
  guard var textToShare = textView.text,
        !textToShare.isEmpty else { return nil }
  if let namePreference
     = UserDefaults.standard.string(forKey: namePreference),
     UserDefaults.standard.bool(forKey: signaturePreference) {
    textToShare += "\n-\(namePreference)"
  }
  return textToShare
}
```

This will create the string that will be shared. If the user has enabled **Include Signature When Sharing** in Settings, the app will append their signature to the text of any entry shared.

Next, replace `share(_:)` with the following:

```
@IBAction private func share(_ sender: Any?) {
  guard let shareText = shareText else { return }
  let activityController
    = UIActivityViewController(activityItems: [shareText],
                              applicationActivities: nil)
  if let popoverController
      = activityController.popoverPresentationController {
    popoverController.barButtonItem
      = navigationItem.rightBarButtonItem
  }
  present(activityController,
          animated: true,
          completion: nil)
}
```

This method will now use the new text that will be generated by `shareText`.

Build and run. Go to Settings and turn on **Include Signature When Sharing**, and enter your name in **Name When Sharing**. Go back to Journalyst, and enter some text in the entry, then select **Action**. You'll be able to see in the preview that your text now includes your name at the end.

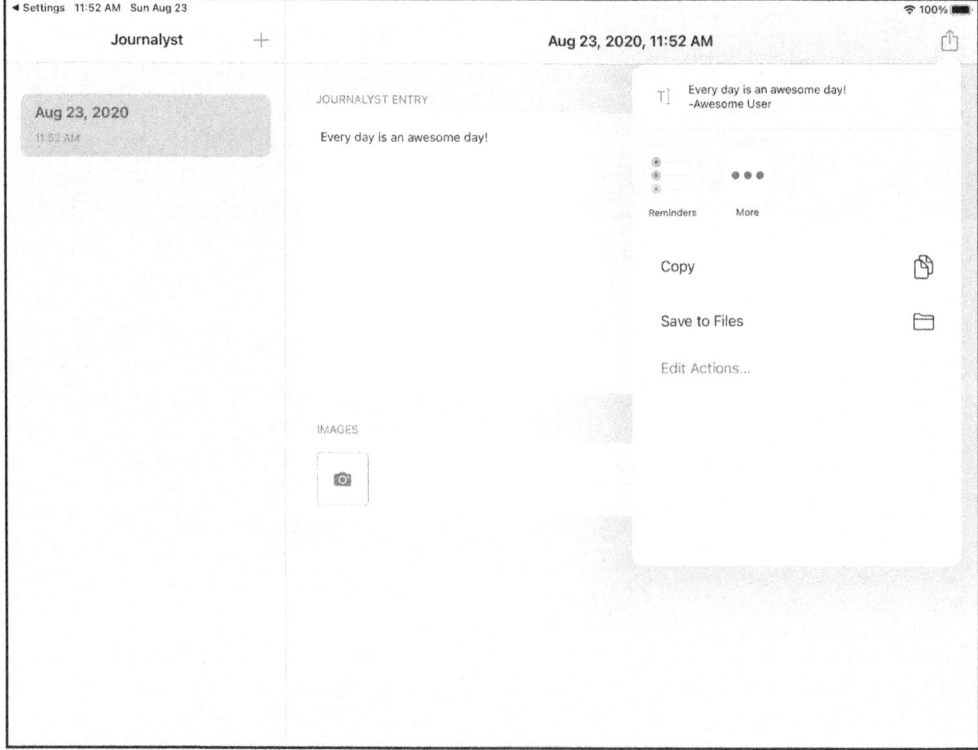

Child panes

Settings.app can do more than just show a simple list of items. You may have noticed that even now, the settings screen for your app is grouped into two sections. You can also add groups and even multiple pages. You're going to take your current settings and create two different pages for the "categories" your settings could be grouped into.

In Xcode, select **File ▸ New ▸ File...**, pick **Property List** and name it **Sharing**. Drag the file *into* **Settings.bundle**:

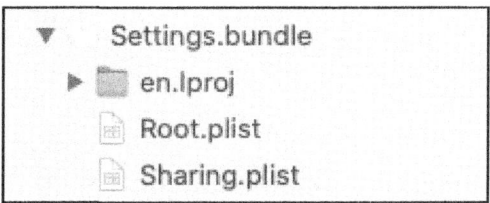

Open **Sharing.plist**, and add the following item:

- **key**: StringsTable

- **value**: Root

> **Note**: In the property list, you can right-click on **Root**, then select **Property List Type ▸ iPhone Settings Plist**. This will let Xcode know that it should show you the appropriate keys and options for a settings bundle. However, it currently will not save the Property List Type after you switch files.

Add another item:

- **key**: PreferenceSpecifiers

- **type**: Array

Click the arrow to the left of the new entry you created and add an array element to it using the plus sign to the right.

> **Note**: When editing a plist, you can use the plus sign to quickly add new items. If you click "plus" next to an item that can't have children, like a string, it will create a sibling entry. If you click "plus" next to an item that *can* have children, it behaves differently depending on whether the current item is "expanded" or "collapsed". When the arrow to the left of the item is pointing right, the item is "collapsed" and the new entry will be a sibling. When the arrow to the left of the item is pointing down, the item is "expanded" and the new entry will be a child.

Change the type of your new entry to **Dictionary** and add the following children:

- **Type**: PSGroupSpecifier

- **Title**: Sharing

This will treat any following items in the list as part of a grouped table view section, with a table view header that says "Sharing".

Next, open **Root.plist**, and highlight **Item 0**, then select **Edit ▸ Cut**. Open **Sharing.plist**, collapse and highlight **Item 0**, and select **Edit ▸ Paste**.

Select the new **Item 0** from **Root.plist**, select **Edit ▸ Cut**, collapse **Item 1** in **Sharing.plist**, and select **Edit ▸ Paste**.

Now, **Sharing.plist** should look like the following:

Key	Type	Value
∨ Root	Dictionary	(2 items)
StringTable	String	Root
∨ PreferenceSpecifiers	Array	(3 items)
∨ Item 0	Dictionary	(2 items)
Type	String	PSGroupSpecifier
Title	String	Sharing
∨ Item 1	Dictionary	(4 items)
Type	String	PSToggleSwitchSpecifier
Title	String	Include Signature When Sharing
Key	String	signature_preference
DefaultValue	Boolean	0
∨ Item 2	Dictionary	(6 items)
Type	String	PSTextFieldSpecifier
Title	String	Name When Sharing
Key	String	name_preference
KeyboardType	String	Alphabet
AutocapitalizationType	String	Words
AutocorrectionType	String	No

Last, back in **Root.plist**, add a new dictionary entry to the end of **Preference Items**. Add the following entries to the dictionary:

- **Type**: Child Pane

- **Title**: Sharing

- **Filename**: Sharing

A Child Pane is an option that allows you to specify the name of another plist within Settings.bundle to navigate to. The Filename value must match the file name that has the settings you want to display, without the extension.

To organize everything more clearly, add two groups to **Root.plist**. In **Root.plist**, select **Preference Items** and then **Editor ▸ Add Item**. Set the following entries on the new dictionary:

- **Type**: Group

- **Title**: Viewing

Next, collapse and select **Item 1** and then choose **Editor ▸ Add Item**. Change dictionary to have only the following entry: **Type**: Group

Root.plist should look like the following:

Key	Type	Value
˅ iPhone Settings Schema	Dictionary	(2 items)
Strings Filename	String	Root
˅ Preference Items	Array	(4 items)
˅ Item 0 (Group - Viewing)	Dictionary	(2 items)
Type	String	Group
Title	String	Viewing
˅ Item 1 (Toggle Switch - Show Entry With Light	Dictionary	(5 items)
Type	String	Toggle Switch
Title	String	Show Entry With Light Background
Description	String	Enable to force a light background on the entry screen.
Identifier	String	entry_color_preference
Default Value	Boolean	NO
˅ Item 2 (Group)	Dictionary	(1 item)
Type	String	Group
˅ Item 3 (Child Pane - Sharing)	Dictionary	(3 items)
Type	String	Child Pane
Title	String	Sharing
Filename	String	Sharing

Build and run, then go to **Settings**. You should now see two entries at the bottom of the settings list. You'll also see how the groups break out the settings more clearly:

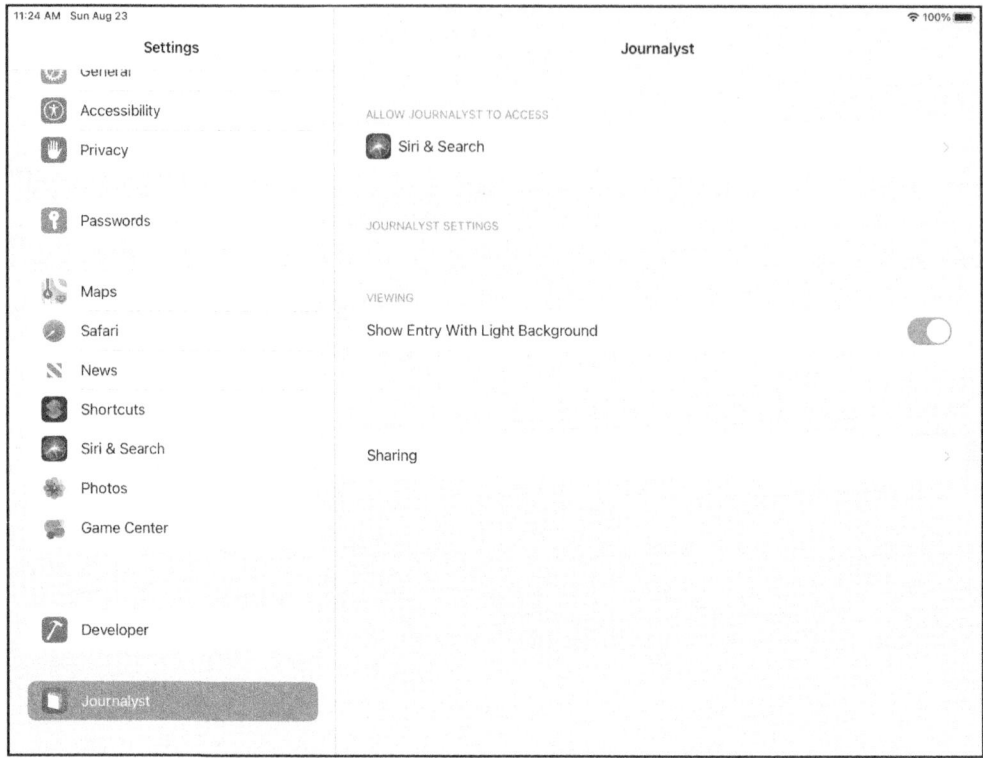

When you select the "Sharing" setting, you'll navigate to another screen where you'll see the specific settings from the corresponding file:

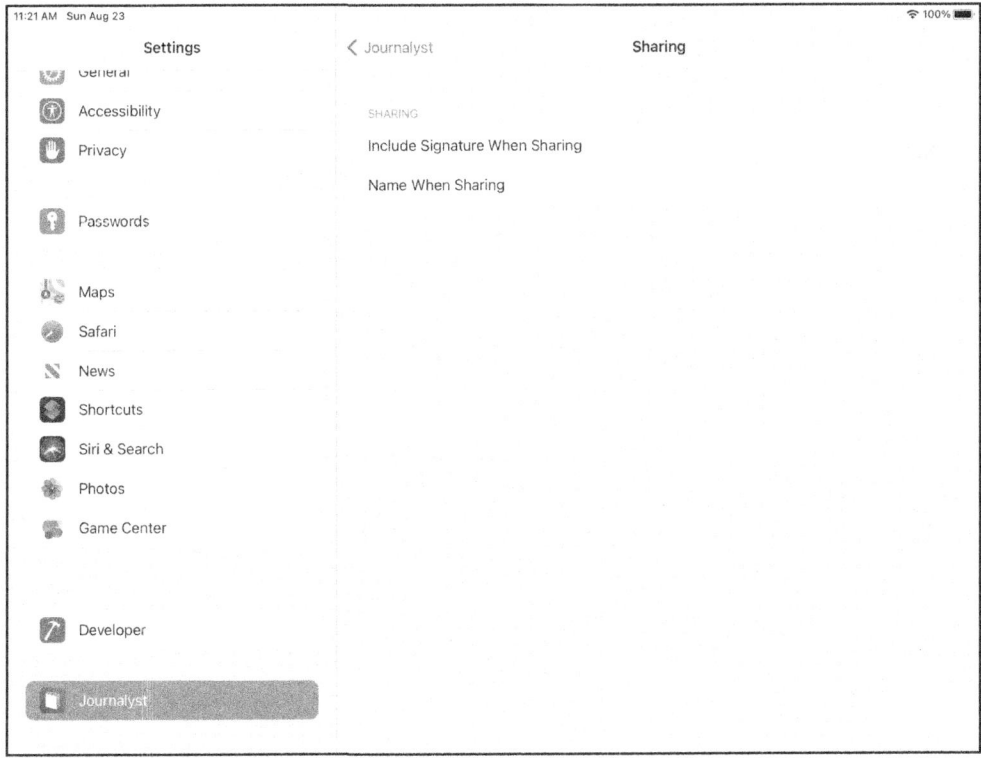

Key Points

- Settings and preferences are helpful for your users.

- Keeping your app's preferences in **Settings.plist** quickly provides a standard way for your users to find available customizations.

- Using multiple plists bring hierarchy and organization to your preferences.

Where to go from here?

You can find out about all the other controls available to you in a settings bundle from Apple's Preferences and Settings Programming Guide. https://developer.apple.com/library/archive/documentation/Cocoa/Conceptual/UserDefaults/Preferences/Preferences.html.

You can also learn about Apple's guidelines for settings in the Human Interface Guidelines. https://developer.apple.com/design/human-interface-guidelines/ios/app-architecture/settings/

Section II: Making a Great Mac App

The good news is that most of your code will be useful for both iPad and Mac platforms. But what about the things that are Mac-specific: like mouse support, Touch Bar support and more?

In this section, you'll take the first-rate iPad app from the previous section and add Mac-specific touches to make it work well on macOS.

Chapter 8: Making Your App Feel at Home on macOS

By Nick Bonatsakis

In the previous section, you learned how to turn your iPhone-only app into a great iPad app. As you now know, this is the first step in making a great Mac app.

In this chapter, you're going to take things to the next level by making some adjustments that will really make your app shine when running on macOS via Catalyst. Throughout the rest of this section, you'll go deeper on several other Mac-specific features. When you're done, you'll have the makings of a world-class Mac app.

By the end of this chapter, you will have learned how to:

- Add a Mac-specific icon.

- Take advantage of system colors.

- Enable window-resizing.

- Enhance your Settings bundle for running on Mac.

- Make a handful of other minor Mac-related improvements.

Until now, you've been test running your app on Mac, but have been focused on iPad. That all changes right now. Ready to finally get your hands dirty with macOS? Fantastic, onward and upward!

It starts with an app icon

One of the first things you might have noticed about running Journalyst on macOS in previous chapters is that it uses the same icon on the Mac as it does on iPhone and iPad. While the icon style as of macOS Big Sur has skewed more towards the rounded rectangle style found on iOS, you still may want to tweak your app icon for macOS. Many of Apple's stock apps now have rounded rectangle icons on macOS, but they are slightly different and distinctly Mac.

Apple has accounted for this fact and given you the ability to include a Mac-specific icon in your app's bundle. And, it's a pretty straight-forward task to do just that.

Open the starter project, then open **Assets.xcassets**. Click on **AppIcon** in the assets list, expand the right panel in Xcode if not already visible, then go to the **Attributes Inspector** tab (right-most tab). Finally, check the checkbox next to **Mac**.

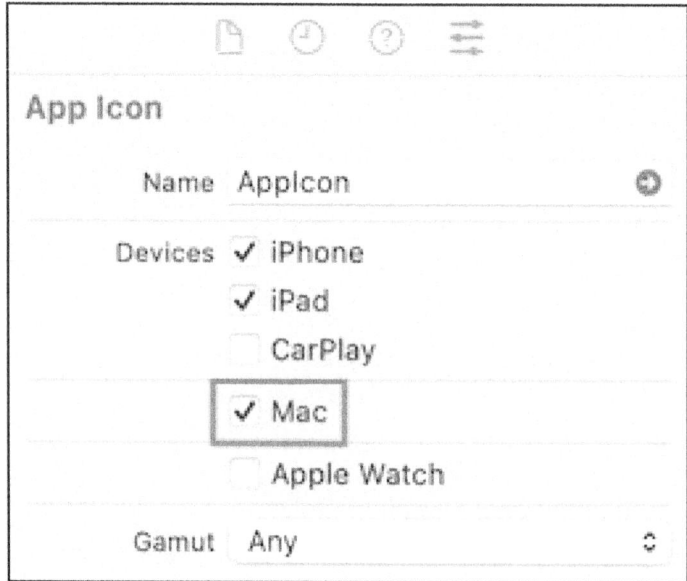

You'll now see several new slots for Mac icon size variants within the main editor. Inside the starter directory for this chapter, you'll find a **Mac App Icon** folder that contains a spiffy new Mac icon in all the required sizes. Drag the appropriately sized icon into each slot to finish up.

Set the target device to **My Mac**, then build and run and you'll find that your app now looks much more at home on the Mac, with an icon that has a larger book glyph.

Adding a touch of color

Another thing you may have noticed when running Journalyst on the Mac is that some of the colors seem off. That's because how iOS uses color differs in some key ways from how it's used on macOS.

Mac apps have traditionally adhered to some precise rules around how and where to use colors for standard system UI elements. Since most Mac apps lean heavily on these elements, they tend to have a very consistent look and feel. Conversely, until now, iOS hasn't exposed system standard colors, and so iOS designs have tended to vary much more in their application of color.

In iOS 13, Apple added a consistent set of "system" colors in the form of static `UIColor` properties. Using these new properties will result in rendered colors that are accurate no matter which OS your app is running on. With this in mind, you're now going to update a few key areas in your app to take advantage of these new colors so that your app adopts Mac-like colors when running on macOS.

The first area that looks somewhat out of place on the Mac is the background of the journal entry's right-hand detail screen. Because its table view uses a grouped style, its background defaults to the `.systemGroupedBackground` color on all OS's. On the Mac, this color renders as white, and this prevents you from differentiating the background from specific element areas.

To fix this, open **EntryTableViewController.swift** and append the following code to `viewDidLoad()`:

```
#if targetEnvironment(macCatalyst)
view.backgroundColor = .secondarySystemBackground
#endif
```

Note the use of `#if targetEnvironment(macCatalyst) ...#endif`.

This is a **compiler directive** enabling you to include code conditionally — here *only* if you're building for the Mac. Within this `#if` block, you then set the view's background color to `.secondarySystemBackground`. The result is a Mac-appropriate off-white background color that's visually distinct from the primary background color.

Next, notice that the journal entry cells in the left-hand sidebar still include lots of colors. On the Mac, data entry cells like this one typically use colored text sparingly. Additionally, the macOS selected color is user-defined and commonly darker than the standard iOS gray color. Together, these issues add up to journal entry cells that look out of place on the Mac.

Open **EntryTableViewCell.swift** and add the following method:

```
private func setupForMac() {
  //1
  dateLabel.textColor = .label
  //2
  dateLabel.highlightedTextColor = .white
  //3
  timeLabel.textColor = .secondaryLabel
  //4
  timeLabel.highlightedTextColor = .white
}
```

Here's what this does:

1. First, you set the normal color for the date label to the `.label` color, which will render as a dark gray in light mode.

2. Next, you set the highlighted text color for the date label to `.white`. This is the color the label changes to when the cell is selected. Most of the time on the Mac, the system-selected color has a higher contrast, so white makes more sense here than on iOS.

3. Now, you set the time label color to `secondaryLabel`. This is a secondary piece of information, so the color provided by the system will be less pronounced than `.label`.

4. Finally, you set the time label highlighted color to `.white` just as you did for the date label.

Now, add the following code to awakeFromNib():

```
#if targetEnvironment(macCatalyst)
setupForMac()
#endif
```

Build and run and you'll find the app looks much nicer now:

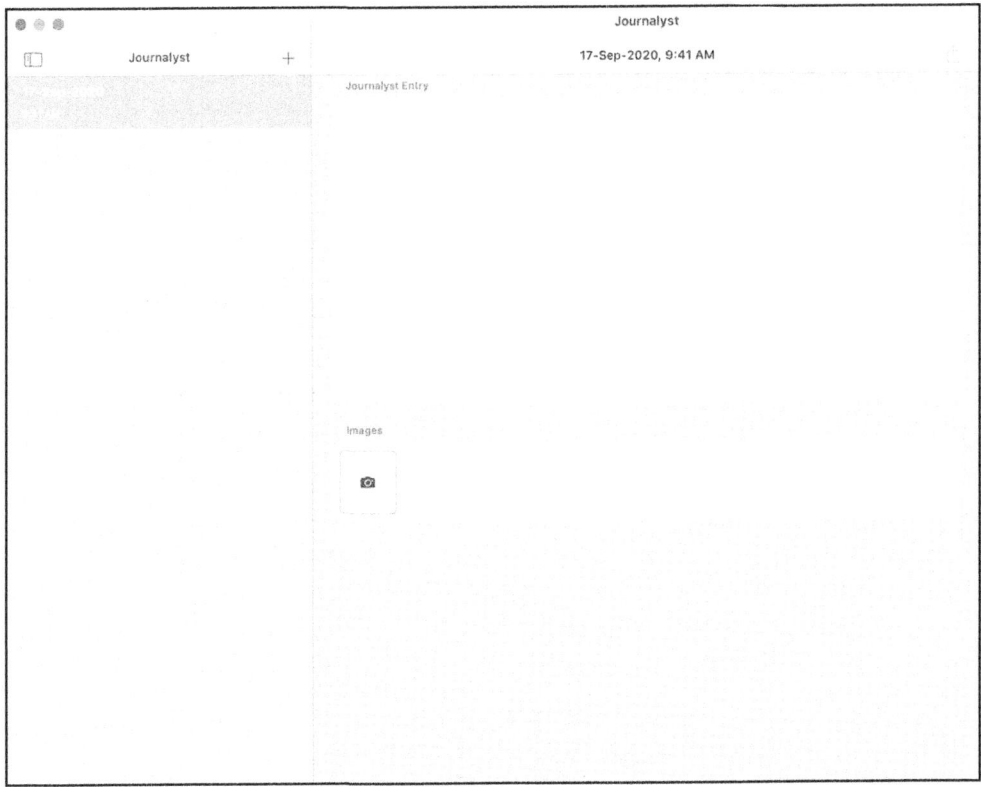

A word on typography

While there is nothing you need to change to make your app's text readable on the Mac, it's worth noting UI content will be scaled down when running on macOS. According to Apple's guidelines.

> Content scaling. Text in the macOS version of an iPad app looks the same as it does in iOS because SF fonts are available on both platforms. However, the baseline font size in iOS is 17 pt, whereas the most common font size in macOS is 13 pt. To ensure that your text and interface elements are consistent with the macOS display environment, iOS views are automatically scaled down to 77%.

Keep this in mind if you have specific situations where this default scaling may cause issues, and take care to address those potential problems.

Sizing down window resizing

When running on an iPad, you have a few options for how a secondary window is sized. On Mac, freeform window sizing has been a platform feature since Apple "borrowed" multi-windowing from Xerox PARC in the 1980s. It would be a shame to let that historical bit of borrowing go to waste, so let's make sure your app supports window resizing properly.

You can already resize the window when running on the Mac, but you'll quickly find that the system doesn't allow you to shrink the window down past a default size. It would be nice to have tighter control over the minimum and maximum window dimensions.

Open **SceneDelegate.swift** and add the following code to the beginning of
`scene(_:willConnectTo:options:)`:

```
if let scene = scene as? UIWindowScene {
  scene.sizeRestrictions?.minimumSize =
    CGSize(width: 768.0, height: 768.0)
  scene.sizeRestrictions?.maximumSize =
    CGSize(
      width: CGFloat.greatestFiniteMagnitude,
      height: CGFloat.greatestFiniteMagnitude
    )
}
```

`sizeRestrictions` is a property on `UIWindowScene` that allows you to control the
minimum and maximum sizes for the window. In the above code, you set the
minimum size to 768x768 and the maximum to
`CGFloat.greatestFiniteMagnitude` which effectively means "as large as you want
to make it."

Now there's one more thing you need to add that will come in handy later on in this
chapter. Add the following notification definition to the top of **SceneDelegate.swift**:

```
extension Notification.Name {
  static var WindowSizeChanged =
Notification.Name("com.raywenderlich.Journalyst.WindowSizeChange
d")
}
```

And then, add the following method to the `SceneDelegate` class:

```
func windowScene(_ windowScene: UIWindowScene,
  didUpdate previousCoordinateSpace: UICoordinateSpace,
  interfaceOrientation previousInterfaceOrientation:
  UIInterfaceOrientation,
  traitCollection previousTraitCollection: UITraitCollection) {
    NotificationCenter.default.post(
      name: .WindowSizeChanged, object: nil)
}
```

The above delegate method gets called whenever the window bounds change. When this happens, you issue the `WindowSizeChanged` notification so that any objects in your app can observe for this event.

Build and run, then try resizing the window. You'll find that the minimum size has now changed to the custom value you specified above. Through the magic of auto-layout, everything looks fine regardless of whatever window size you ultimately choose.

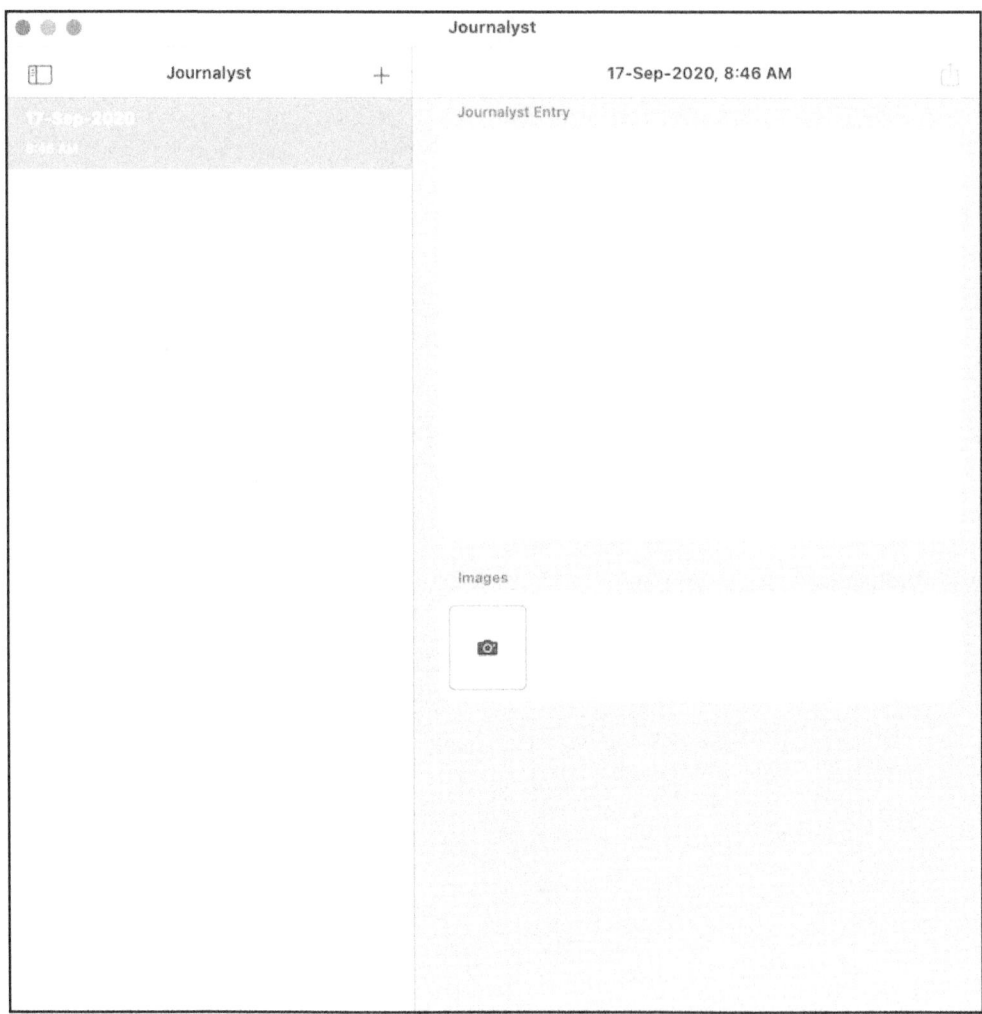

Preferential treatment

In the previous section, you learned how to add a Settings bundle to expose app preferences to the iOS Settings app. By doing so, you also enabled a default *Preferences* window for your app when running on the Mac, accessible via the **Journalyst ▸ Preferences** menu item. The out-of-the-box screen looks like this:

Not too bad, especially for free. But you can do better!

First, you'll notice that both tabs use the same default icon. The default icon is fine for the *General* tab, but it'd be nice to have a separate icon for the *Sharing* tab. Thankfully, the Settings bundle mechanism now supports adding custom icons, so that you can add some style.

To start things off, find **sharing.png** and **sharing@2x.png** in **starter/Sharing Settings Tab Icon**, and drop them into the top level of **Settings.bundle**. Then, to specify the icon for the *Sharing* tab, do the following:

1. Find **Sharing.plist** inside the Settings bundle and open it.

2. Right-click on the Root element and click **Add Row**.

3. Set the key for the new row to `Icon`.

4. Finally, set the value to `sharing`.

It's pretty common for Mac preference panes to have descriptions for checkbox-based settings. Your current app lacks these descriptions, so you'll add them to both boolean settings.

To add the description on the *General* tab:

1. Open **Root.plist** in the Settings bundle.

2. Expand **Preference Items** and then expand **Item 1**.

3. Right-click **Item 1** and click **Add Row**.

4. Set the key to `Description`.

5. Set the value to `Enable to force a light background on the entry screen`.

Now, add a description to the checkbox on the *Sharing* tab:

1. Open **Sharing.plist** in the Settings bundle.

2. Expand **PreferenceSpecifiers** and then expand **Item 1**.

3. Right-click **Item 1** and click **Add Row**.

4. Set the key to `Description`.

5. Set the value to `Automatically include a custom signature when sharing journal entries.`

The last preference enhancement you're going to add is to show a confirmation prompt when the user turns on the journal entry signature setting on the *Sharing* tab. This is another feature that is specific to apps running on the Mac, so the plist entries will be ignored when running on iOS.

To add the confirmation dialog:

1. Open **Sharing.plist** in the Settings bundle.

2. Expand **PreferenceSpecifiers** and then expand **Item 1**.

3. Right-click **Item 1** and click **Add Row**.

4. Set the key to `TrueConfirmationPrompt`.

5. Set the type to `Dictionary`.

Add the following sub-items as `String` key value pairs to `TrueConfirmationPrompt`, again by right-clicking and then choosing **Add Row** for each:

*   `Type -> PSConfirmationPrompt`

*   `Title -> Confirm Share Name`

*   `Prompt -> Turning this on will share your name with the journal entry`

*   `ConfirmText -> Enable`

*   `DenyText -> Don't Enable`

Now, **Build and run**. Then, open the preferences pane by clicking **Journalyst ▸ Preferences**. Your hard work has paid off, and you now have a much more Mac-like preferences window. Try enabling and disabling the various settings to see how things work.

Pretty slick right? Just a few more odds and ends to take care of and you'll be on your way.

A few more odds and ends

Another thing that may be nagging your better Mac sensibilities is the look of the sidebar. On Mac, sidebars for split views tend to be styled in such a way that they let the content beneath bleed through, applying a blur.

Adding this behavior to your split view's side bar is a simple one-liner. Open up **RootSplitViewController.swift** and append the following to the end of `viewDidLoad()`:

```
splitViewController.primaryBackgroundStyle = .sidebar
```

That one line of code will keep the sidebar unchanged on iOS, but when running on the Mac, it will now look like the standard macOS sidebar.

Next, you have a minor scrollbar-related tweak to make. As you learned back in Chapter 1, when any `UIScrollView` instance is used, and your app is running on the Mac, the scroll bars that are only visible on demand on iOS are styled as Mac scrollbars and visible at all times. E.g., when someone is actively scrolling.

> **Note:** By default scrollbars will auto-hide on Mac when using a trackpad. You may not experience any scrollbar related issues if you have this setting enabled in System Preferences and don't use a mouse. If you'd like to see what it looks like for your users who use a mouse, open System Preferences, choose General, and under the "Show scroll bars" setting, choose "Always".

On the journal entry detail screen, the images appear in a `UICollectionView` that is laid out horizontally. On iOS, the scroll bars aren't really necessary, since the way the list extends off the side of the screen makes it pretty apparent that it is a scrollable element. But on the Mac, there's no touch interaction, so scrollbars are how you typically move the content area.

Open **EntryTableViewController.swift** and update the `#if targetEnvironment(macCatalyst)` code block at the end of `viewDidLoad` to match this:

```
#if targetEnvironment(macCatalyst)
view.backgroundColor = .secondarySystemBackground
collectionView.showsHorizontalScrollIndicator = true
#endif
```

Now, when running on the Mac, the collection view that renders images will have a scrollbar visible if the content extends past the view frame. That's not quite enough to make this work. You still need to let the collection view know when the window bounds change, or else it won't know to update the scrollbar state. For example, if you start with a window that is very wide and can accommodate all the images, but then resize to a much smaller window width, the collection view needs to change from not showing scrollbars to showing them.

Remember the `WindowSizeChanged` notification you added to `SceneDelegate` earlier in this chapter? It's time to make use of it!

Still in **EntryTableViewController.swift**, add the following code to `viewDidLoad()`:

```
NotificationCenter.default.addObserver(
  self,
  selector: #selector(handleWindowSizeChanged),
  name: .WindowSizeChanged,
  object: nil
)
```

The above code should be pretty familiar, as you have done many times already. You are subscribing to a notification, in this case, `WindowSizeChanged`.

Next, add the implementation for the `handleWindowSizeChanged()` handler method like so:

```
@objc func handleWindowSizeChanged() {
  collectionView.reloadData()
}
```

This will force the collection view to reconsider whether it should be showing scrollbars or not, based on its current bounds.

Lastly, there is one more minor tweak you'll want to make to how sidebar cells are rendered. At present, whenever you make changes to the text of a journal entry, the sidebar cell shows a preview of that text. This looks fine on an iPad, where cell heights commonly vary, but on the Mac, they tend to be more uniform, so it would be nice not to show that text preview in this case.

Open **EntryTableViewCell.swift** and add the following code to the `didSet` of the `entry` property:

```
#if targetEnvironment(macCatalyst)
summaryLabel.isHidden = true
#endif
```

Pretty straight-forward! You're again using the `#if` `targetEnvironment(macCatalyst)` check to only run the code when on the Mac, in this case, hiding the summary label.

Build and run one more time, then bask in the glory that is your app, one huge step closer to being a marvelously Mac-like macOS app. Try saying that ten times fast!

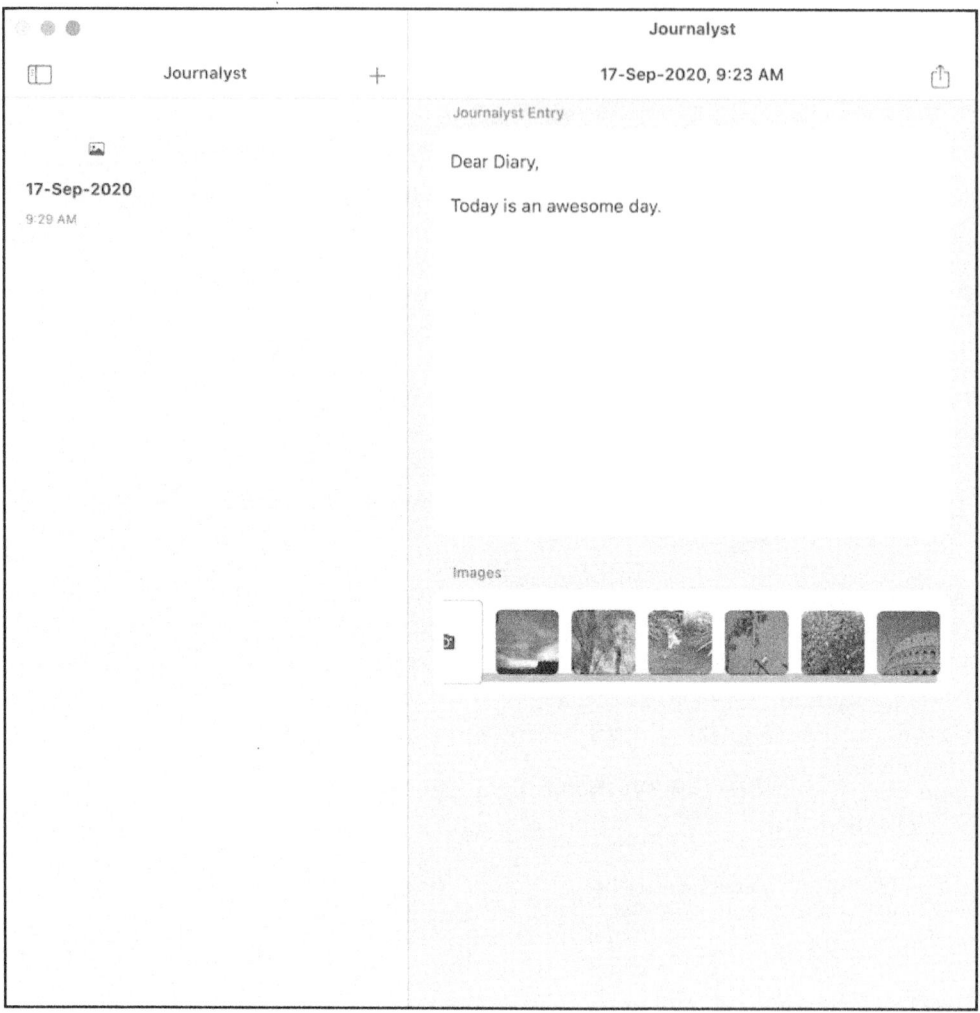

Key points

- Including a Mac-specific icon for your Catalyst app is easy and helps make the app feel more at home on the Mac.

- There are many ways to leverage system colors to improve the styling of your iOS app when it runs on the Mac.

- You need to consider window resizing when your app runs on the Mac.

- Mac preferences panels get lots of functionality for free for Catalyst apps, but you can go further with some extra effort.

Where to go from here?

In this chapter, you took the first steps towards really making your iOS app shine when running macOS, taking advantage of various styling methods, window resizing, preferences, and more. But there are still some glaring omissions, things you'd expect to see in a great Mac app.

In the next chapter, you're going to learn how to replace those navigation bars that look so out of place on the Mac, with native Mac toolbars.

Chapter 9: The Mouse

By Andy Pereira

Just like a keyboard, the mouse is a toolset that you may not have encountered if you've focused solely on iOS development. Catalyst makes working with the mouse easy since it provides a familiar pattern, and it gives you a great amount of control in the process.

In this chapter, you'll learn how to implement `PointerStyleProvider` and `UIHoverGestureRecognizer`. You'll take a look at the differences between iOS/iPadOS and touch targets in macOS.

Getting started

Open the starter project for this chapter. Build and run for iPadOS. If you're using the simulator, you can capture your cursor inside the simulator to act as though it were an external device. Do this by selecting **Capture Pointer** in the simulator toolbar:

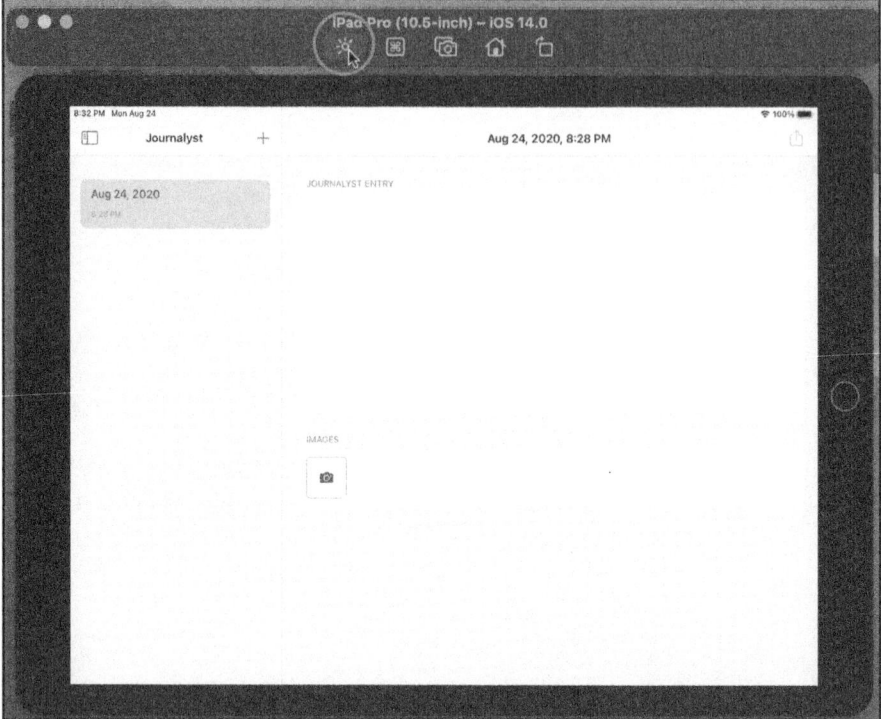

Add a few entries and then move your mouse around the app. Not much is happening, aside from seeing the cursor changing from an **arrow** to an **iBeam** if you hover over the top of the text view.

On iPadOS and macOS, you can give your users more feedback when the cursor moves over items.

Pointer style providers

On iPadOS, your cursor is going to behave a bit different from that of macOS. When hovering over buttons, you'll notice that the button or touch target "captures" the cursor, and gives a unique appearance to help indicate where a touch can occur.

Open **EntryTableViewController** and the following block of code inside
`supplementaryDataSource()`, just before the line that returns `reusableView`:

```
if let button = reusableView.viewWithTag(1) as? UIButton {
  button.pointerStyleProvider = { button, effect, _ in
    var rect = button.bounds
    rect = button.convert(rect, to:
effect.preview.target.container)
    return UIPointerStyle(effect: effect,
shape: .roundedRect(rect))
  }
}
```

Here, you've added a very simple `UIButton.PointerStyleProvider`. Added in iOS
13.4, it allows you to define custom styles and shapes for your cursor on touch areas.
Here, you simply take the button's shape, have the pointer style take the entire shape
of it.

Build and run, and capture the mouse. Then hover your mouse over the Camera
button to see the effect take place. You should see the button fill with a color, like
below:

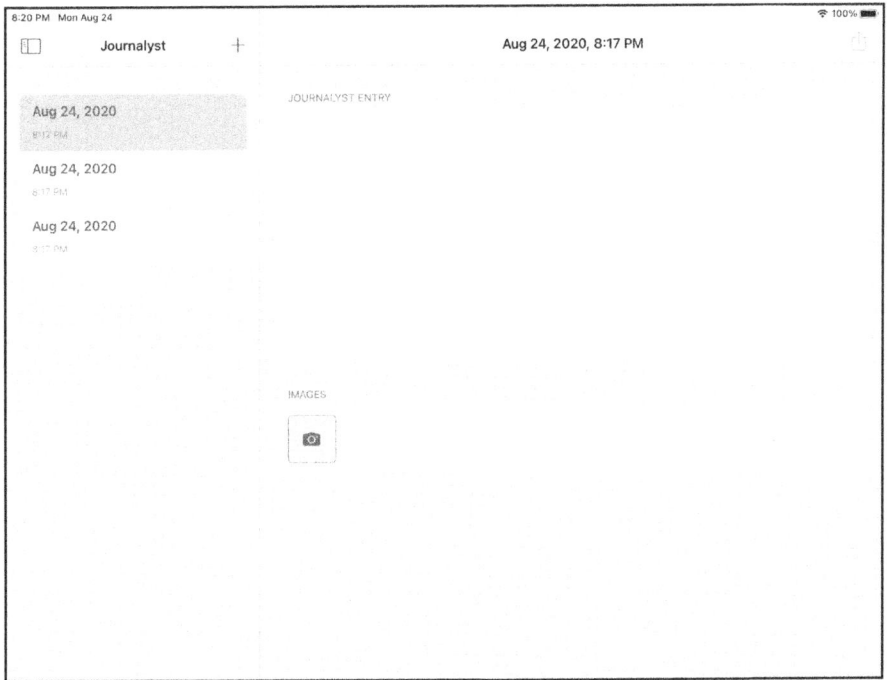

It is a subtle effect, but things like this make a difference to your users, even if they
aren't thinking about it.

Adding effects with hover gesture recognizer

Next, you'll use `UIHoverGestureRecognizer` to add some more effects for iPadOS, as well as macOS.

To start, open **EntryTableViewCell.swift**. Add the following to the end of `awakeFromNib()`.

```
addHoverGesture()
```

Then add the following method to the class:

```
private func addHoverGesture() {
  let hoverGesture
    = UIHoverGestureRecognizer(target: self,
                               action: #selector(hovering(_:)))
  contentView.addGestureRecognizer(hoverGesture)
}
```

This method does the following:

- It creates a hover gesture recognizer, setting `self` as the target, and an action that you'll set up in the next step.

- It adds the hover gesture to the content view of the cell.

Next, add the following to the same class:

```
@objc private func hovering(_ recognizer:
UIHoverGestureRecognizer) {
  // 1
  guard !isSelected else { return }
  // 2
  switch recognizer.state {
  // 3
  case .began, .changed:
    backgroundColor = .secondarySystemBackground
  // 4
  case .ended:
    backgroundColor = .none
  default:
    break
  }
}
```

Here, you can see how you respond to the hover events:

1. This ensures that nothing happens if you've already selected the cell.

2. The gesture recognizer passes itself as a parameter to this method. You check the state of the gesture recognizer.

3. If the hover is starting (i.e., .began) or moving around (i.e., .changed), you change the background color of the cell.

4. Once the mouse is no longer hovering over the view (i.e., .ended), you remove the color you set.

Build and run the app. Then add a few entries and hover your mouse over the table view. You should now see that all the cells, except for the cell you selected, change background color while the mouse is over it. Once the mouse leaves the view, it changes back to having no background color.

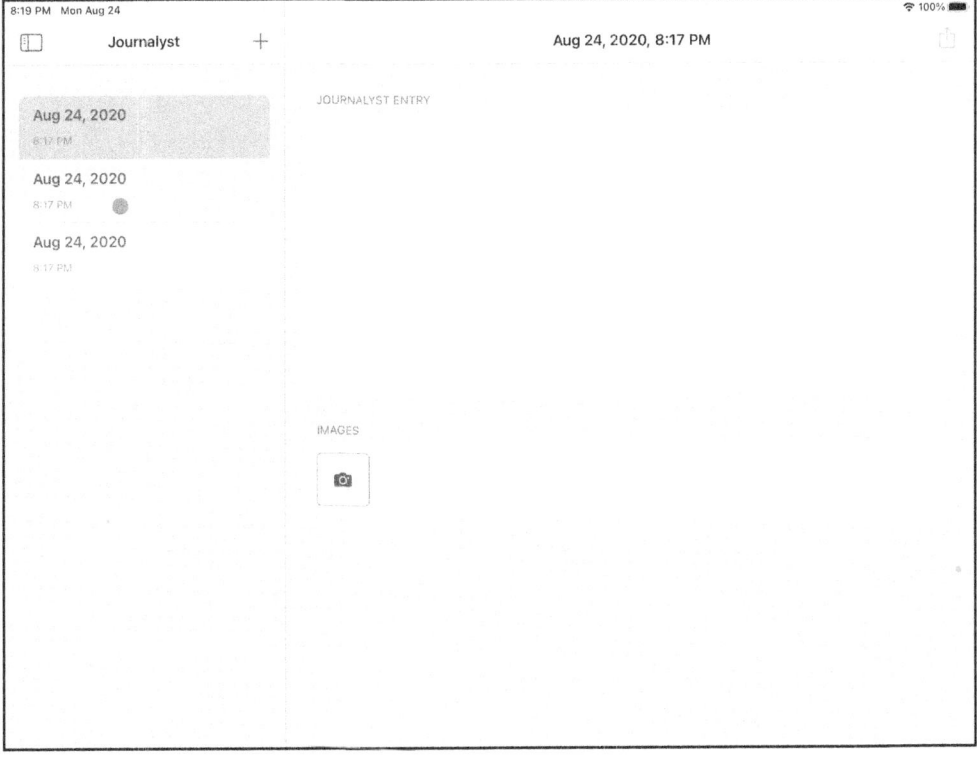

There's one more place where you can add a hover gesture to give your app more finesse.

Open **EntryTableViewController.swift** and add the following to `supplementaryDataSource()`, just before it returns `reusableView`:

```
let hoverGesture
  = UIHoverGestureRecognizer(target: self,
      action: #selector(self.hovering(_:)))
reusableView.addGestureRecognizer(hoverGesture)
```

Once again, this code creates a hover gesture and adds it to the reusable view that the collection view's header returns.

Next, add the following method to the class:

```
@objc private func hovering(_ recognizer:
UIHoverGestureRecognizer) {
  #if targetEnvironment(macCatalyst)
  switch recognizer.state {
  case .began, .changed:
    NSCursor.pointingHand.set()
  case .ended:
    NSCursor.arrow.set()
  default:
    break
  }
  #endif
}
```

Here, you respond to the event over the Add Image button and change the cursor to the pointing hand when above it. It will go back to the default arrow when you mouse away from it. While this code you added in the first section was only for iPadOS, this new code will complement your UI on macOS, all without having to write too much code.

Build and run on macOS. Then hover over the Camera button in the Entry view. It should now change cursor shapes as you mouse over it.

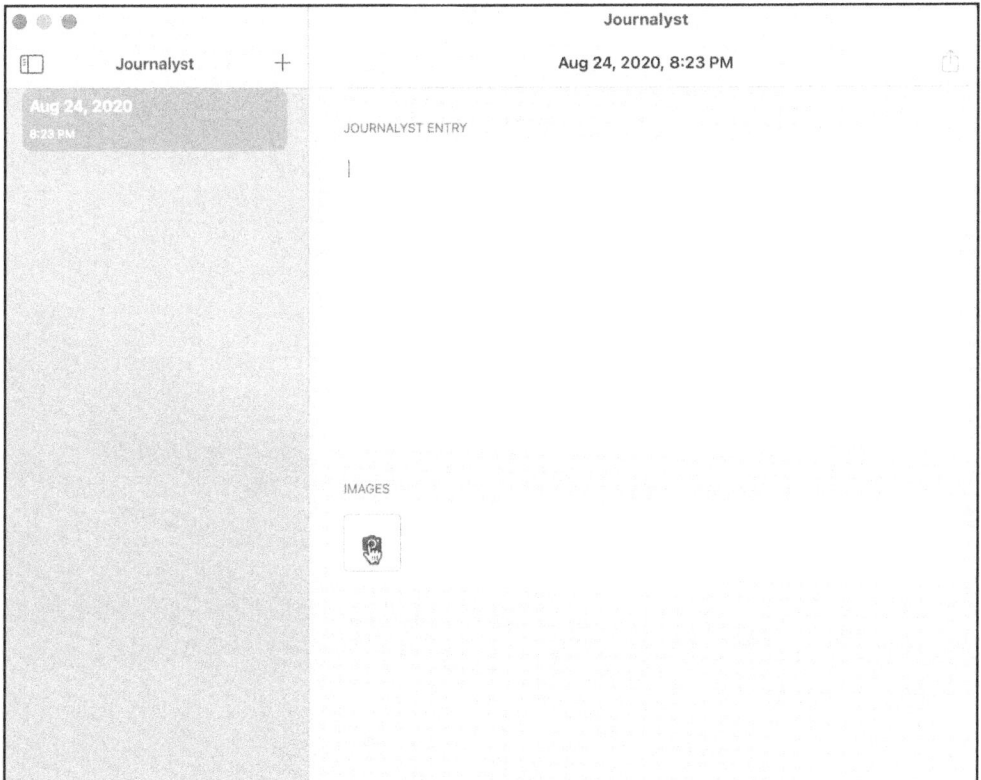

A few notes on elements and haptics

Keep in mind that the interface guidelines for iOS state that you should keep touch targets for interactive elements to a minimum of 44pt × 44pt. The cursor gives you a lot more flexibility when your app is running on macOS. If you're creating macOS-specific UI elements, you can use smaller elements if it makes sense for your app.

You also have access to haptic feedback on both platforms. You could easily set up haptic feedback when mousing over an area if your app requires it. Keep Apple's guidelines in mind, and remember not to overstimulate your users.

Bridging the gap

In a previous edition of this book, some frameworks or tools that were available in macOS were not available in Mac Catalyst, like NSCursor. While NSCursor has been added now, if you find yourself needing to utilize some other components, you can create an AppKit bundle. Creating a bundle and accessing its contents is out of the scope of this book, but here are some pointers:

- Only embed the bundle in macOS.

- You need to create a class in the bundle and make it the **Principal Class**. This is done inside the **Info.plist** of the bundle.

- While *possible* in Swift, you may find that Objective-C is a bit easier for loading classes, and calling code dynamically.

Working with bundles in this manner can be challenging, especially if you are unfamiliar with it. You may find it is worth going down this path if you need access to something, or you may be content waiting for Apple to provide the missing piece later down the road.

You can read more about bundles from Apple's bundle programming guide, here: https://developer.apple.com/library/archive/documentation/CoreFoundation/Conceptual/CFBundles/Introduction/Introduction.html

Key points

- You can use `PointerStyleProvider` to respond to cursor events on iPadOS.

- Add hovering to views by adding a hover gesture recognizer to give your user more visual feedback.

- Hover gesture recognizers work similarly to other gesture recognizers.

- You can access `NSCursor` on macOS with Catalyst.

- Bundles may provide a solution to missing functionality.

Where to go from here?

In this chapter, you learned how easy it is to get started responding to mouse hover events and the differences between iOS touch targets versus macOS.

You can find Apple's Human Interface Guidelines for the mouse and trackpad, here: https://developer.apple.com/design/human-interface-guidelines/macos/user-interaction/mouse-and-trackpad/.

You can read more about `UIHoverGestureRecognizer` from Apple's website: https://developer.apple.com/documentation/uikit/uihovergesturerecognizer.

To learn more about the possible states for a gesture recognizer, refer to the following Apple documentation: https://developer.apple.com/documentation/uikit/uigesturerecognizer/state.

Chapter 10: Barista Training: Menu Bar

By Marin Benčević

Welcome to barista training! In the next few chapters, you'll learn all about adding different kinds of bars to your Catalyst app, including the menu bar, toolbars and supporting the touch bar. In this chapter, you'll trim the default menu bar of the Journalyst app to remove some unnecessary items. You'll also add new items to delete, share and add new entries. Get out your beans and your fancy hipster oat milk — it's time to get brewing!

A free menu bar

All Catalyst apps include a default menu bar for free. Open up the starter project from the provided materials and run it on macOS. When your app is active, you'll see its menu bar at the top of your screen. All the standard menus like *File*, *Edit*, etc. are already there.

Apple sometimes calls the menu bar the "main menu." That's how you should think about what actions to put in the menu bar. Like in a video game, the main menu includes general actions the user can perform inside your app.

One thing you should keep in mind is that menu bars aren't dynamic. They're built once when the app launches and the items never change during runtime. For more dynamic actions related to specific parts of your app, use context menus as described in Chapter 5, "Adding Some Context."

The menu bar itself is a nested `UIMenu` instance. Each `UIMenu` can contain child menus and **commands**. Commands are the buttons you can press to do something. They can be enabled or disabled, and each command can specify a keyboard shortcut for easier access.

Commands get executed using something called the **responder chain**.

The responder chain

Open the **Edit** menu, and you'll notice that *Cut*, *Copy* and *Paste* are all greyed out. This makes sense: Since nothing is selected, there's nothing to cut or copy.

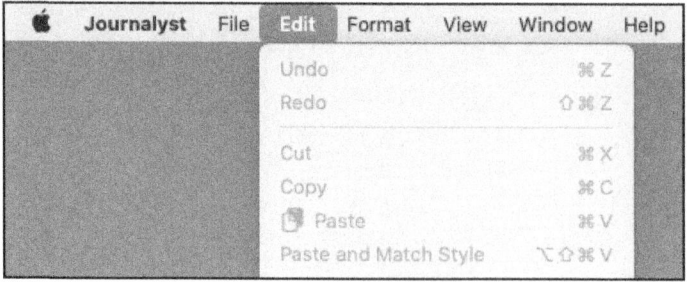

However, if you type in something in the entry screen and select the text, you'll notice the menu items are now enabled.

UIKit disables and enables these items for you using the **responder chain**. The responder chain is built up of UIResponder instances, which include all views, view controllers and the app itself.

When you click on the text view, it becomes the **first responder**. The responder chain starts from the text view and moves up the view hierarchy through all superviews and view controllers, all the way to the app itself.

Menu items use the responder chain to enable or disable themselves. Each menu item has an associated **selector**. When the first responder changes, menu items query the whole responder chain to see if anyone can perform their selector. In the case of *Cut*, the text view can perform the action. *File ▸ Close* is always active because the app handles that one, and the app is always at the far end of the responder chain.

OK, that's enough theory for one day. It's time to get hacking.

Beyond the default menu

You'll start by trimming some unnecessary items from the menu bar. The menu bar can be changed either in Interface Builder or through code. In this section, you'll use Interface Builder and, later in the chapter, you'll learn how to do the same in code.

Open **Main.storyboard**, from the **Library** drag over a **Main Menu** anywhere on the storyboard. You should see a new scene in the storyboard that looks just like your menu bar:

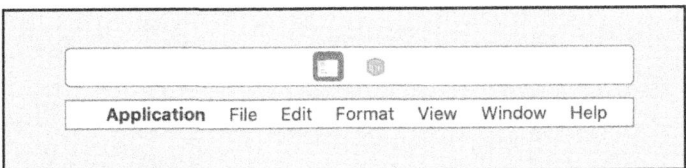

Select the **Format** menu in the sidebar and press **Command-Backspace** to delete it. Since you're not using rich text in the app, this menu serves no purpose. Build and run the project, and you should see a menu bar without *Format*:

Now, add a new command for adding new entries. Start by going back to the Library and dragging over an **Inline Section Menu** to the top of the **File** menu in the Outline View.

This adds an **inline menu** with two commands. Inline menus can't be opened. Instead, all of their commands are added to the parent menu, separated with a thin line from other items.

Select **Item 1** and open the Attributes inspector. Change the Title to **New Entry**. Then click the Key Equivalent box and press **Option-Command-N**. This adds a keyboard shortcut to the command.

Next, in **RootSplitViewController.swift** add the @IBAction attribute for addEntry(sender:) at the start of it's declaration. It should look like this:

```
@IBAction @objc private func addEntry(sender: UIKeyCommand) {
```

Then return to the storyboard again, control-drag from the **New Entry** command to the **first responder**, which is the little yellow cube above the menu bar in the storyboard. Select `addEntryWithSender:` as the sent action.

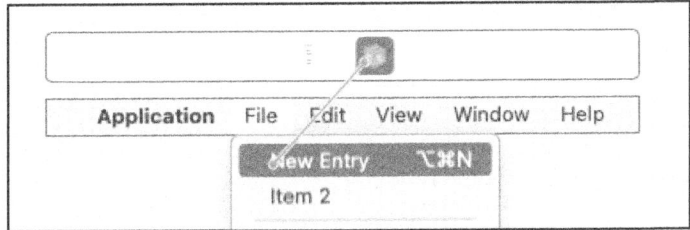

This connects the `addEntryWithSender:` selector to the command. As discussed earlier, the system will search the responder chain until it finds an object which can perform that selector.

If the function weren't marked as `@IBAction`, Interface Builder would not be able to find the function.

Build and run the project, select the current entry in the side bar and then select **File ▸ New Entry** in the menu bar. You'll see a new entry pop up. You can also press **Option-Command-N** to add new items.

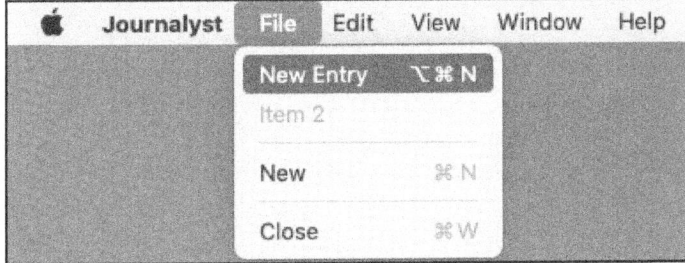

Congrats, young barista, you just brewed your first menu item. Let's keep the momentum going by adding a command to delete an entry.

Deleting entries

Back in **Main.storyboard**, select **Item 2** in the File submenu you added earlier. In the Attributes Inspector, change its **Title** to **Delete Entry** and set the **Key Equivalent** to **Shift-Command-Backspace**.

Open **RootSplitViewController.swift** and add `@IBAction` to
`removeEntry(sender:)`:

```
@IBAction @objc private func removeEntry(sender: UIKeyCommand) {
```

Again, the function needs to be annotated with `@IBAction` so interface builder can
see it.

Now, back in **Main.storyboard** control-drag from the **Delete Entry** command to the
first responder and select `removeEntryWithSender:` as the action.

Build and run the project and select the first entry. Select **File ▸ Delete Entry** to
delete the entry.

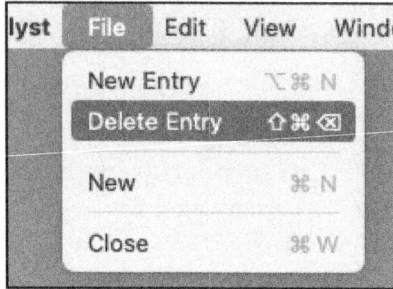

It might be a good idea to give the user more information about *which* item they're
deleting. You can do that by changing the command's title to include the date and
time of the currently selected entry.

Open **RootSplitViewController.swift** and add the following override to the class,
right after `removeEntry`:

```
// 1
override func validate(_ command: UICommand) {
  // 2
  switch command.action {
  case #selector(removeEntry):
    // 3
    if let mainNavigationController =
viewController(for: .primary)
        as? UINavigationController,
        let mainTableViewController =
mainNavigationController.topViewController
        as? MainTableViewController,
        let selectedIndexPath =
mainTableViewController.tableView.indexPathForSelectedRow {
        // 4
        let entry =
DataService.shared.allEntries[selectedIndexPath.row]
```

```
        command.title = "Delete \(entry.dateCreated)"
    } else {
        // 4
        command.title = "Delete Entry"
    }
default:
    break
    }
}
```

This code is densely packed with information, so here's a break-down of what's going on:

1. The `validate` function gets called for each command the view controller can perform actions for, and it gives you a chance to update the command's look.

2. You're only interested in the command for deleting entries, so you check that its selector matches `deleteEntry`.

3. Fetch the split view controller's master, grab the main table view controller and its selected index path.

4. If there's a selected entry, change the command's title to include the date and time of the entry.

5. Otherwise, change its title back to *Delete Entry*.

Build and run the project. If you open up the **File** menu with an entry selected, you'll see its date and time in the command's title.

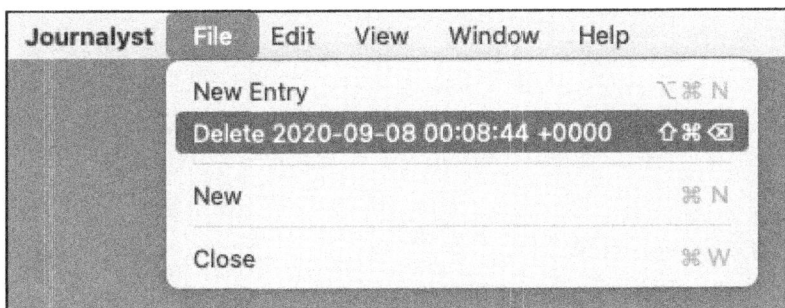

That's a hot cup of freshly ground UX improvements served to your users!

> **Note:** The responder chain can sometimes behave in unexpected ways and commands might get disabled for no apparent reason. You can combat this by calling `becomeFirstResponder` on the view you want to focus on, and even *that* is not guaranteed to always work. The responder chain can be quite fickle!

Next, you'll add a command for sharing entries, but this time it's not going to be in Interface Builder.

Sharing entries

The menu bar is only one of the potentially many menus you can have in your app. Each `UIResponder` can add or remove items from their menus. The responder that's responsible for the menu bar is the application itself, or in other words, the app delegate.

Open up **AppDelegate.swift** and override the following function in the class:

```
override func buildMenu(with builder: UIMenuBuilder) {
}
```

This overrides a `UIResponder` method responsible for adding and removing items from menus. Since you're only interested in changing the menu bar, add the following check to the function:

```
guard builder.system == .main else { return }
```

You'll build up a new inline menu that will contain a command to share an entry. Start by adding the following code that creates the command to the end of the function:

```
let shareCommand = UIKeyCommand(
  title: "Share",
  action: #selector(EntryTableViewController.share),
  input: "s",
  modifierFlags: [.command])
```

You use a `UIKeyCommand` so that you can attach a keyboard shortcut to the command. This will call it *Share* and give it a keyboard shortcut of *Command-S*. Once it's pressed, the selector it should call is `share` implemented in `RootSplitViewController`.

Next, create the menu that contains the command by adding this bit of code to the end of the function:

```
let shareMenu = UIMenu(
  title: "",
  options: [.displayInline],
  children: [shareCommand])
```

Since the menu's options say that it's displayed inline, the title won't get shown, so you can leave it empty. The menu only has one child: The share command you created earlier.

Finally, it's time to use the builder to add the item to the menu bar. Add this line to the end of the function:

```
builder.insertChild(shareMenu, atStartOfMenu: .file)
```

You can specify exactly where your item goes. In this case, add it to the start of the *File* menu.

UIKit doesn't call `buildMenu` if there's an initial menu specified in the storyboard. To get around this issue, disable the main menu in the storyboard:

1. Open **Main.storyboard**.

2. Select **Main Menu**.

3. In the **Attributes Inspector** uncheck **Is Initial Menu**.

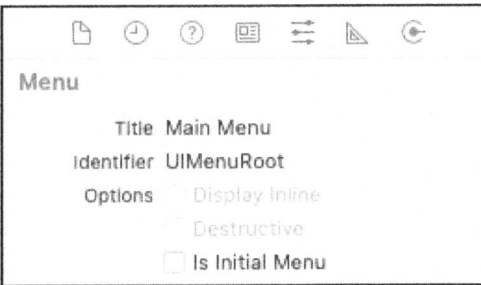

This makes Main Menu *not* the main menu, and makes sure the app calls `buildMenu` at launch. Of course, the items you added in the storyboard won't be visible anymore.

Build and run the project. Select an entry and type something in the log. You can now select **File ▸ Share** to open up the share sheet. You can also do this by pressing **Command-S**.

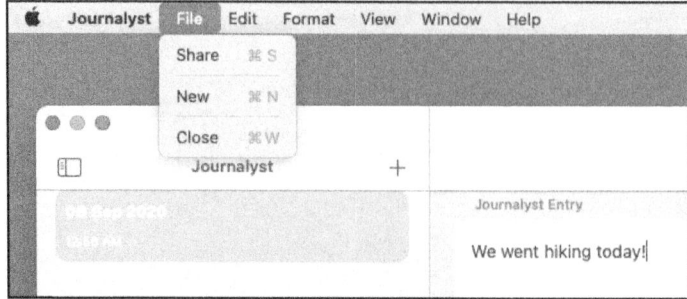

One final issue with the menu bar is that the *Share* item is enabled even if the log is completely empty. There's no point in sharing an empty string, so you're going to disable the menu bar in that case.

Open **EntryTableViewController.swift** and override `validate(_:)` once again:

```
override func validate(_ command: UICommand) {
  switch command.action {
  case #selector(share):
    if textView.text.isEmpty {
      command.attributes = [.disabled]
    } else {
      command.attributes = []
    }
  default:
    break
  }
}
```

If the user hasn't entered any text, you're going to add `.disabled` to the command's attributes array. Otherwise, you're going to clear the attributes so that the command becomes enabled.

> **Note:** You can also disable commands by overriding `canPerformAction` and returning `false`. Keep in mind that by doing so, `validate` won't get called for the disabled command.

Build and run the project one last time and you'll see *Share* disabled until you type something into the entry's text view.

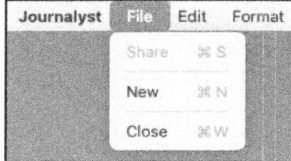

This concludes your barista training for the menu bar! Keep an eye out for any cafe managers hitting you up with job offers.

Key points

- Catalyst apps include a default menu bar for free.

- The menu bar consists of nested **menus** which contain **commands**.

- Each command has a **selector** that it calls when pressed, and uses the **responder chain** to enable and disable itself.

- You add or remove items from the menu bar by dragging over a **Main Menu** to your app's storyboard.

- You can make the same changes in code by overriding `buildMenu` in the app delegate.

- Override `validate` in a `UIResponder` subclass to change the appearance of a command.

Where to go from here?

The Human Interface Guidelines section on menus (apple.co/2EymXZv) has some useful tips of which actions to consider for the menu bar, and where to put them.

To see which options you have when building out a menu bar, check out the documentation for `UIMenuBuilder` here: apple.co/33lcUyj. You can also see the different properties of `UICommand` to get a sense of how to further customize commands: apple.co/2M6qJvp.

Finally, the WWDC 2019 session "Taking iPad Apps for Mac to the Next Level" walks you through building a menu bar using the menu builder: apple.co/33j3CmM.

Chapter 11: Barista Training: Toolbar

By Andy Pereira

Toolbars are an essential part of macOS applications. Without a doubt, NSToolbar is used so ubiquitously across so many apps that most users may overlook its presence. Because of this, it's essential to understand what you get when you use a toolbar and how toolbars behave. By adopting NSToolbar in your app, you have access to almost two decades worth of work from the smart developers and designers at Apple.

Getting started

Open the starter project for this chapter. Select **My Mac** for the active scheme, and Build and run. At the moment, this project has a split view controller and can handle multiple windows:

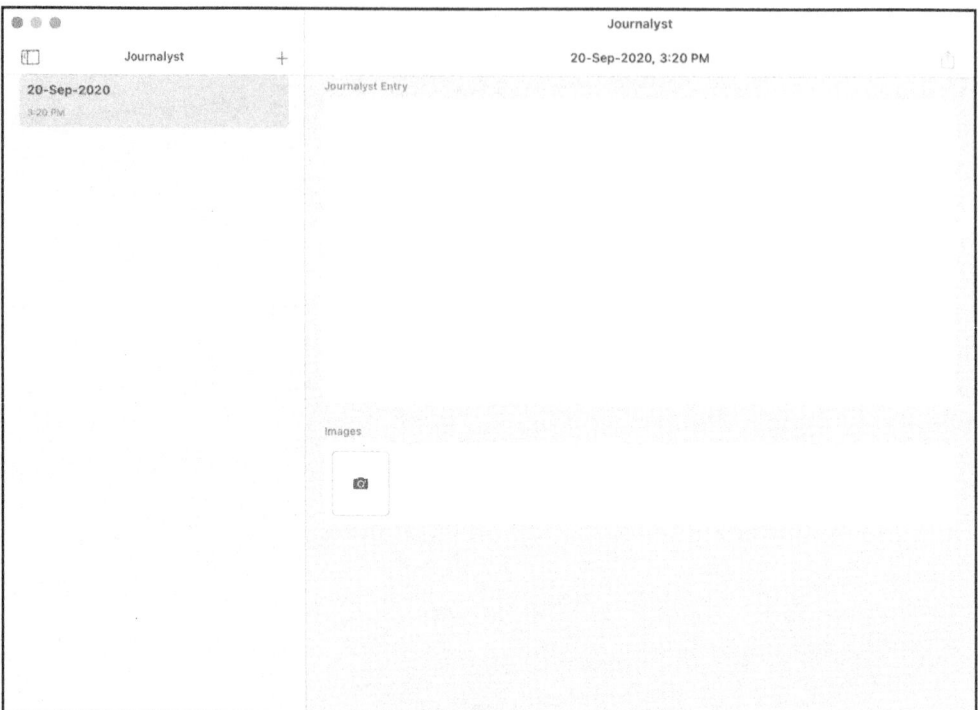

Adding the toolbar

NSToolbar is a macOS-specific control. In the past, you probably had to use macros or targets to ensure frameworks did not get imported into unsupported builds. With Catalyst, you'll need to be able to integrate your macOS, iOS and iPadOS code more seamlessly.

To add the toolbar, open **SceneDelegate.swift** and add the following to the end of
scene(_:willConnectTo:options:):

```
#if targetEnvironment(macCatalyst)
// 1
if let scene = scene as? UIWindowScene,
  let titlebar = scene.titlebar {
  // 2
  let toolbar = NSToolbar(identifier: "Toolbar")
  // 3
  titlebar.toolbar = toolbar
}
#endif
```

Here's what you've done:

1. You check that the scene has a titlebar. This property will be present if the app
    is running inside of a macOS environment.

2. Then you create a toolbar with an identifier. Every one of the toolbars will have
    the same identifier so that the system synchronizes their state across windows.

3. Last, you set the toolbar on the titlebar.

Build and run, and you'll see a beautiful — albeit empty — toolbar.

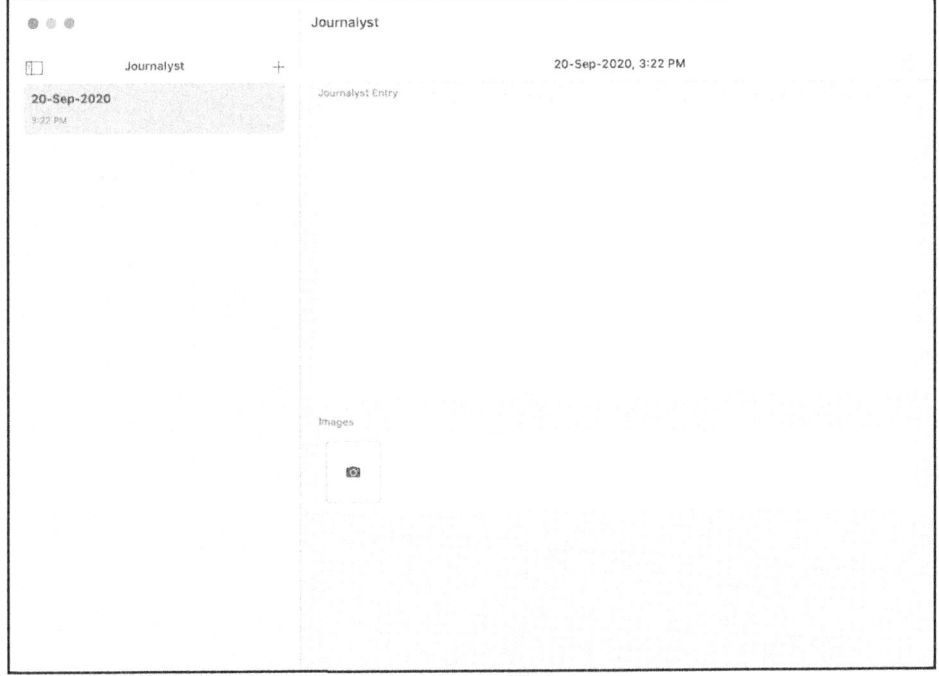

It doesn't make sense to keep the navigation bars around any longer, as the toolbar will serve the same purpose.

To get rid of both of the navigation bars, open **MainTableViewController.swift** and add the following to the end of `viewDidLoad()`:

```
#if targetEnvironment(macCatalyst)
navigationController?.navigationBar.isHidden = true
#endif
```

Then, open **EntryTableViewController.swift** and add the same line of code to the existing macro. Build and run, and now your navigation bars are gone, leaving just a toolbar:

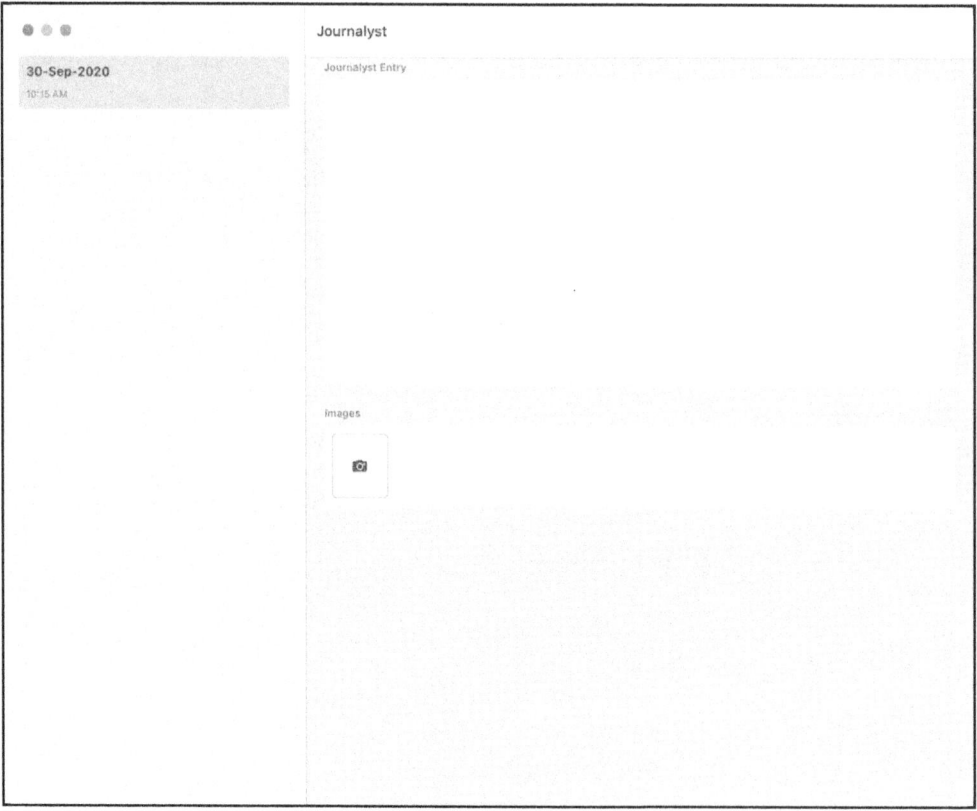

Adding buttons

In its current state, the toolbar is providing no functionality to the app. To start adding functionality, you'll be adding a few buttons.

Open **SceneDelegate.swift** and add the following after setting the toolbar on the titlebar:

```
toolbar.delegate = self
```

Next, at the end of the file, inside the empty macro that checks for Catalyst, add the following:

```
extension NSToolbarItem.Identifier {
  static let addEntry =
    NSToolbarItem.Identifier(rawValue: "AddEntry")
  static let deleteEntry =
    NSToolbarItem.Identifier(rawValue: "DeleteEntry")
  static let shareEntry =
    NSToolbarItem.Identifier(rawValue: "ShareEntry")
}

extension SceneDelegate: NSToolbarDelegate {
}
```

These three toolbar identifiers are needed to start adding buttons to the toolbar. Just like you added an identifier to the toolbar for the system to know how to sync across windows, these identifiers allow the toolbar to know *what* is added to itself.

Next, add the following to the **NSToolbarDelegate** extension:

```
func toolbarAllowedItemIdentifiers(_ toolbar: NSToolbar)
  -> [NSToolbarItem.Identifier] {
    return
  [.toggleSidebar, .addEntry, .deleteEntry, .shareEntry, .flexible
  Space]
}
```

By adding this, you tell the toolbar which identifiers are allowed to be in the toolbar. You'll notice that the three identifiers are what you added above.

The first item, `.toggleSidebar` is a convenience button for showing and hiding your sidebar. The last one, `.flexibleSpace`, is a system-defined identifier that places a blank item that used to automatically adjust its spacing. As of macOS 11, it just adds a divider line.

Now, add the following method:

```
func toolbarDefaultItemIdentifiers(_ toolbar: NSToolbar)
  -> [NSToolbarItem.Identifier] {
  return [.toggleSidebar, .addEntry, .shareEntry]
}
```

Adding `toolbarDefaultItemIdentifiers(_:)` will inform the toolbar what should initially be displayed in itself. Also, later on, when you start customizing the toolbar, it will provide the user a way to reset the toolbar to the initial state.

You're almost there, but there are a few more steps before you can add the buttons. Add the following methods inside the same extension:

```
// 1.
func toolbar(_ toolbar: NSToolbar,
  itemForItemIdentifier itemIdentifier:
  NSToolbarItem.Identifier,
  willBeInsertedIntoToolbar flag: Bool) -> NSToolbarItem? {
    var item: NSToolbarItem?
    return item
}

// 2.
@objc private func addEntry() {
}

@objc private func deleteEntry() {
}
```

Here's what you've added:

1. This method will provide the actual buttons to a toolbar. It is currently incomplete and will be finished shortly.

2. These methods are for convenience right now and will be finished later.

At last, you're ready to add the buttons.

Add the following property to `SceneDelegate`:

```
#if targetEnvironment(macCatalyst)
private let shareItem =
  NSSharingServicePickerToolbarItem(itemIdentifier: .shareEntry)
#endif
```

Replace `toolbar(_:itemForItemIdentifier:willBeInsertedIntoToolbar:)` with the following:

```
func toolbar(_ toolbar: NSToolbar,
  itemForItemIdentifier itemIdentifier:
  NSToolbarItem.Identifier,
  willBeInsertedIntoToolbar flag: Bool) -> NSToolbarItem? {

  var item: NSToolbarItem?
  switch itemIdentifier {
  case .addEntry:
    item = NSToolbarItem(itemIdentifier: .addEntry)
    item?.image = UIImage(systemName: "plus")
    item?.label = "Add"
    item?.toolTip = "Add Entry"
    item?.target = self
    item?.action = #selector(addEntry)
  case .deleteEntry:
    item = NSToolbarItem(itemIdentifier: .deleteEntry)
    item?.image = UIImage(systemName: "trash")
    item?.label = "Delete"
    item?.toolTip = "Delete Entry"
    item?.target = self
    item?.action = #selector(deleteEntry)
  case .shareEntry:
    return shareItem
  case .toggleSidebar:
    item = NSToolbarItem(itemIdentifier: itemIdentifier)
  default:
    item = nil
  }
  return item
}
```

You add custom buttons to the toolbar by checking the identifier passed in and returning the appropriate button. Here are the buttons you added:

1. **Add**: This will add a new journal entry to the app.

2. **Delete**: Based on the active window, it will delete the selected entry.

3. **Share**: Just like delete, it will share the active window's current entry.

Build and run. Because your default buttons are just **Add** and **Share**, you will only see two buttons on the right initially:

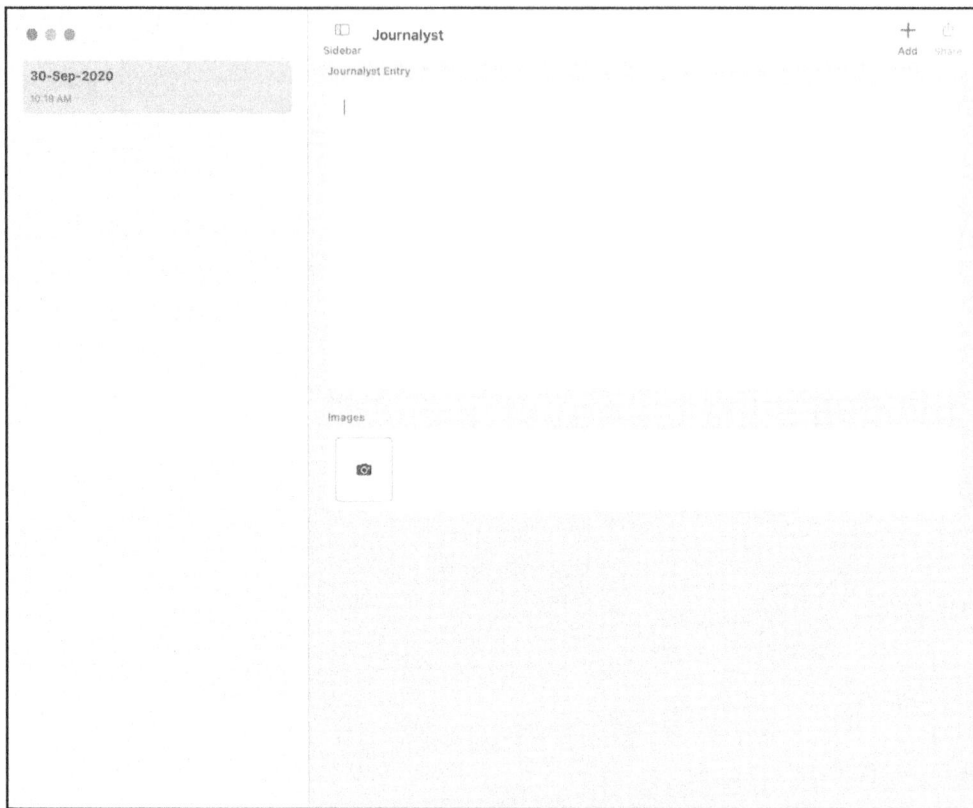

OK. You're now officially past the hardest part of working with toolbars in this tutorial!

Customizing the toolbar

Toolbars don't always have to contain a fixed set of buttons. Above, you provided a delete button without giving the user a way to see it. You can enable your toolbar to be customized by the user, and save its state between launches.

Still within **SceneDelegate.swift**, add the following lines of code after you set the delegate for the toolbar inside of `scene(_:willConectTo:options:)`:

```
toolbar.allowsUserCustomization = true
toolbar.autosavesConfiguration = true
```

By setting `allowsUserCustomization`, you enable users to customize their toolbar by right-clicking on it. Also, `autosavesConfiguration` will determine if the system should save the toolbar configuration to `NSUserDefaults`, persisting the user's preferences between runs.

Build and run, then right-click on your toolbar. You'll see an option to **Customize Toolbar**:

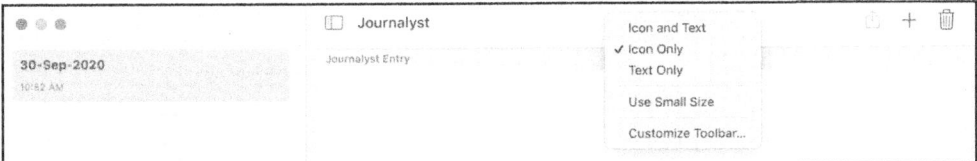

Select this option, and you'll see a modal window in which you can customize the toolbar:

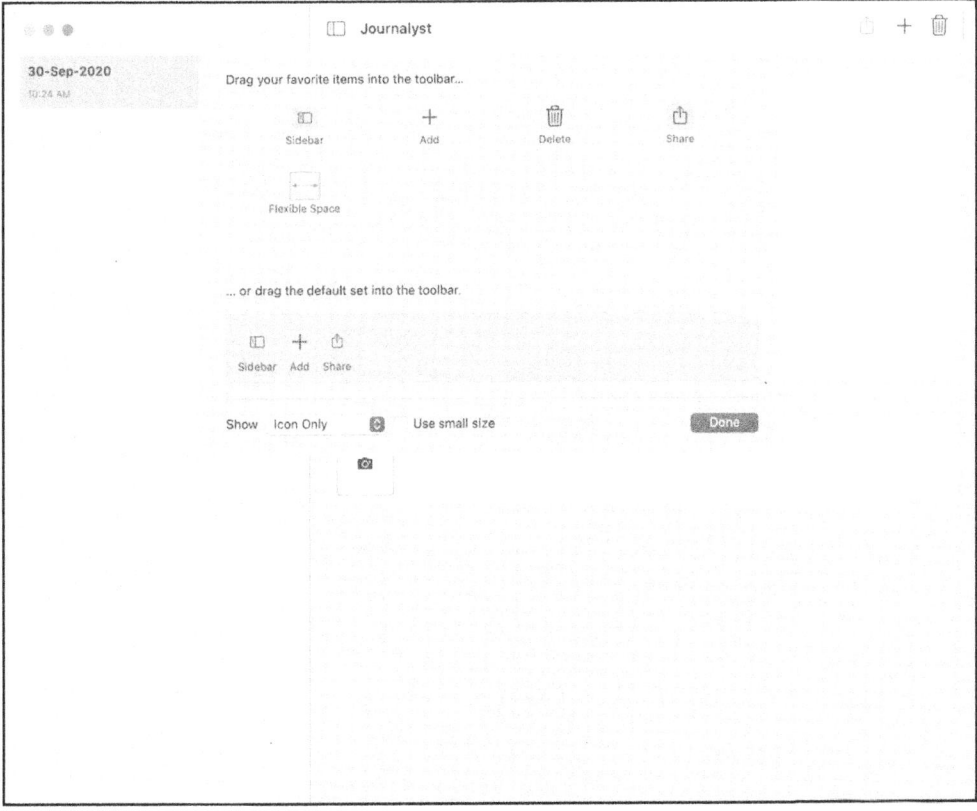

Try changing the configuration, then quit the application and restart it. Your changes should remain between runs.

Finally, you can also remove the title bar from the window, making the toolbar a bit smaller. To test this, add the following to `scene(_:willConnectTo:options:)`, after setting the delegate:

```
titlebar.titleVisibility = .hidden
```

Build and run to see how this looks:

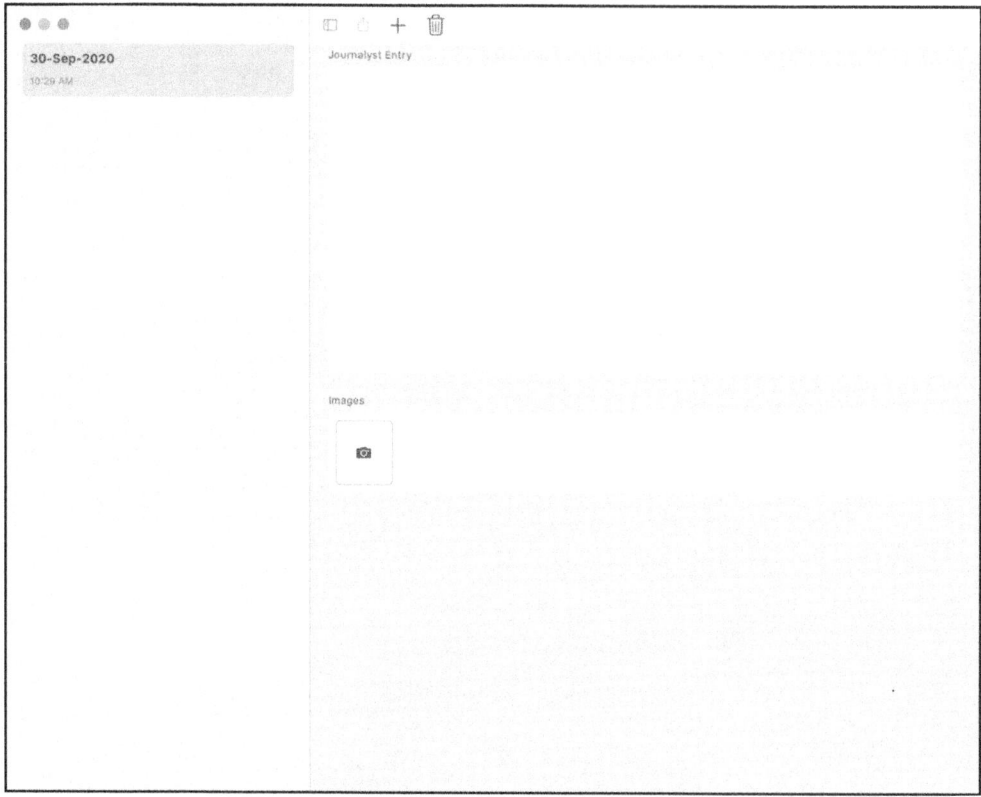

Notice that the labels and the title in the window are now gone. You can remove this line of code for the remainder of the tutorial.

Responding to actions

The last thing you need to do is respond to actions in the toolbar. To add items to the list, replace the empty implementation of `addEntry()` with the following:

```
@objc private func addEntry() {
  guard
```

```
    let splitViewController
      = window?.rootViewController
      as? UISplitViewController,
    let navigationController
      = splitViewController.viewControllers.first
      as? UINavigationController,
    let mainTableViewController
      = navigationController.topViewController
      as? MainTableViewController else {
    return
  }
  DataService.shared.addEntry(Entry())
  let index = DataService.shared.allEntries.count - 1
  mainTableViewController.selectEntryAtIndex(index)
}
```

This code will add a new entry to your data model, and then select it in the list.

Build and run, then select **Add**. You should see entries get added to the list:

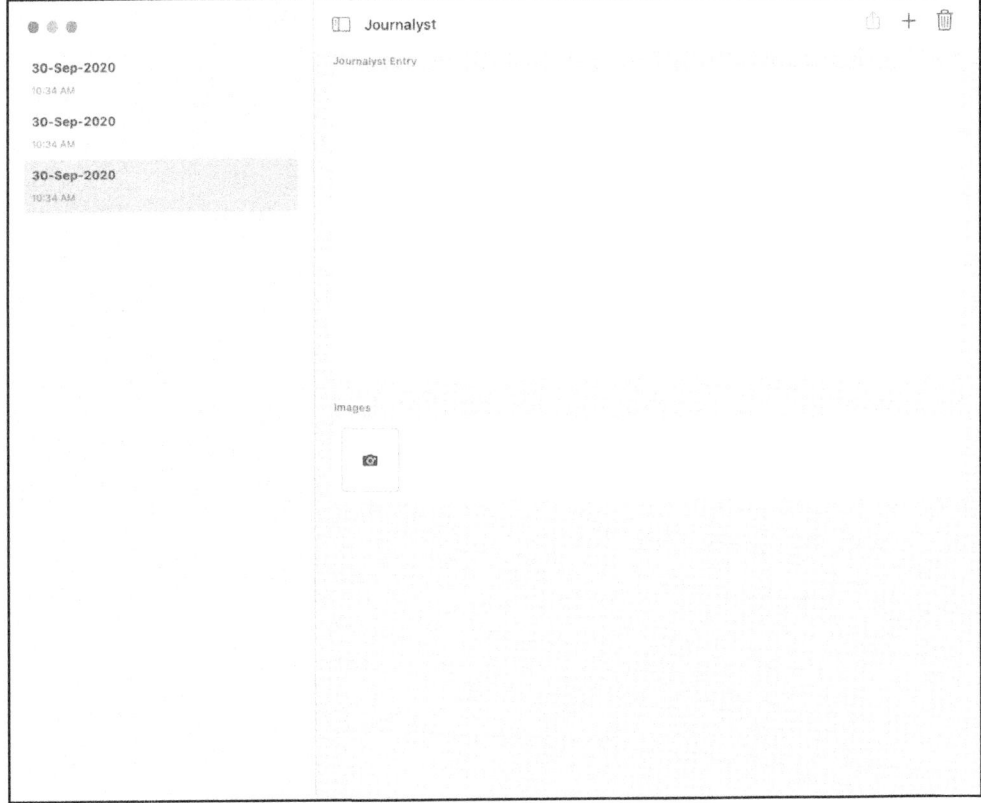

Next, implement `deleteEntry()` with the following:

```
guard let splitViewController =
  window?.rootViewController as? UISplitViewController,
  let navigationController =
    splitViewController.viewControllers.first
    as? UINavigationController,
  let mainTableViewController =
    navigationController.topViewController
    as? MainTableViewController,
  let secondaryViewController =
    splitViewController.viewControllers.last
    as? UINavigationController,
  let entryTableViewController =
    secondaryViewController.topViewController
    as? EntryTableViewController,
  let entry = entryTableViewController.entry,
  let index = DataService.shared.allEntries
    .firstIndex(of: entry) else { return }
DataService.shared.removeEntry(atIndex: index)
mainTableViewController.selectEntryAtIndex(index)
```

This isn't as complicated as it may first appear. Because your app can have multiple windows, you need to check which entry is selected in the window you select **Delete** in. This code simply goes through the hierarchy of the active window and removes the appropriate entry.

Build and run. Ensure you have the delete button in your toolbar, add a few entries, then select **Delete**.

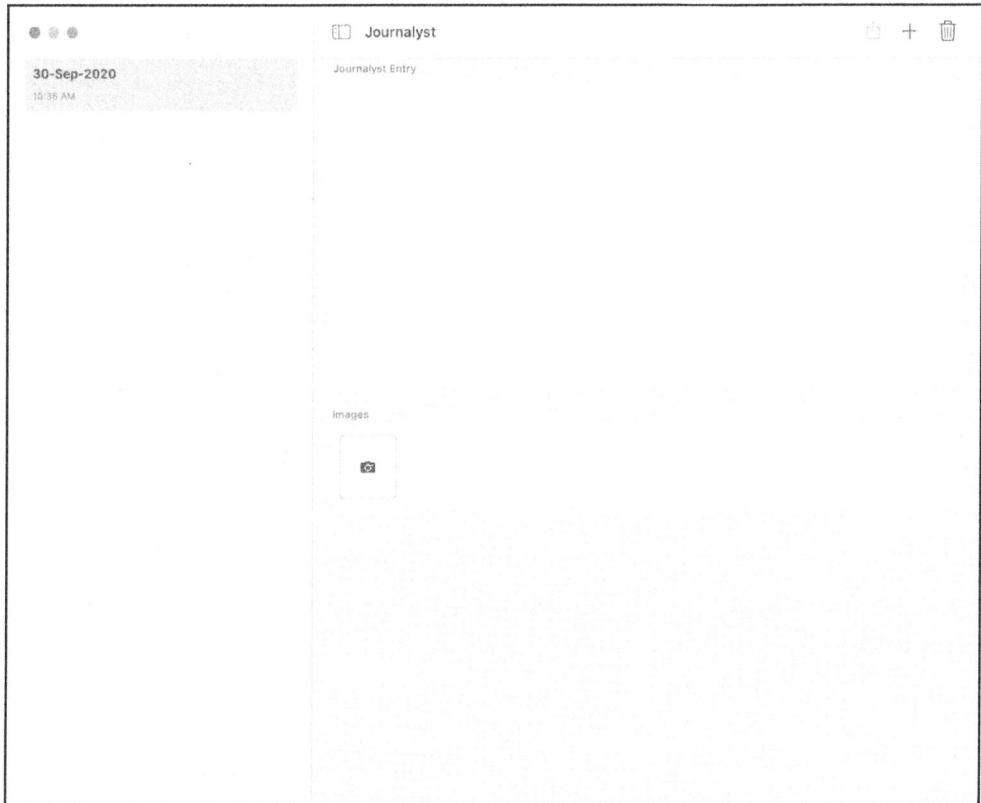

Sharing

For the final toolbar item, **Share**, you'll need to do a few more steps. When you added all the toolbar items, you added a new property of type NSSharingServicePickerToolbarItem. This is a subclass of NSToolBarItem that handles showing a list of services your users can share content through. To get this working takes a few steps.

First, import Combine in **SceneDelegate.swift**:

```
import Combine
```

Next, add a new property to `SceneDelegate`:

```
private var activityItemsConfigurationSubscriber:
AnyCancellable?
```

This property will listen for notifications that will be sent when entries are selected in the main list, or as text is entered for an entry. To setup the subscription, add the following in **SceneDelegate.swift**, after the lines of code you set the delegate for the toolbar inside of `scene(_:willConectTo:options:)`:

```
activityItemsConfigurationSubscriber
  = NotificationCenter.default
  .publisher(for: .ActivityItemsConfigurationDidChange)
  .receive(on: RunLoop.main)
  .map({
      $0.userInfo?[NotificationKey.activityItemsConfiguration]
        as? UIActivityItemsConfiguration
  })
  .assign(to: \.activityItemsConfiguration,
          on: shareItem)
```

If you're unfamiliar with **Combine**, all you need to understand is the following:

- You setup `activityItemsConfigurationSubscriber` to listen for the notification `ActivityItemsConfigurationDidChange`.

- When it receives the notification, handle any actions on the main thread.

- Grab the `activityItemsConfiguration` that was sent in the notification, and assign it to your **Share** button's `activityItemsConfiguration`.

At the moment, your **Share** item is always disabled. It should remain disabled until an entry is in a state to be shared.

To handle this behavior, and setup the configuration that your button is expecting, open **EntryTableViewController.swift** and add the following extension to the end of the file:

```
extension EntryTableViewController {
  private func configureActivityItems() {
    let configuration
      = UIActivityItemsConfiguration(objects: [])
    // 1.
    configuration.metadataProvider = { key in
      // 2.
      guard let shareText
            = self.shareText else { return nil }
      switch key {
```

```
      // 3.
      case .title, .messageBody:
        return shareText
      default:
        return nil
      }
    }
    // 4.
    NotificationCenter
      .default
      .post(name: .ActivityItemsConfigurationDidChange,
            object: self,
            userInfo: [NotificationKey
                         .activityItemsConfiguration:
  configuration])
    }
}
```

Here's a breakdown of what you've added:

1. You create a `UIActivityItemsConfiguration` and setup what needs to be provided through the `metadataProvider`. This will inform the service that handles sharing your content what needs to be shared.

2. Ensure that you have text to share, otherwise don't allow content to be shared.

3. Set your entry's text as the content to be shared.

4. Post a notification with the new configuration. This is the notification and configuration content you setup in the previous step.

There's two places you'll want to call `configureActivityItems()`. First, add the following to the main body of `EntryTableViewController`:

```
override func viewDidAppear(_ animated: Bool) {
  super.viewDidAppear(animated)
  configureActivityItems()
}
```

This will handle notifying your toolbar item to update whenever you switch entries.

Finally, replace `textViewDidChange(_:)` with the following:

```
func textViewDidChange(_ textView: UITextView) {
  validateState()
  configureActivityItems()
}
```

Now, when you start entering any text for an entry, the share button will be updated with your latest content.

Build and run, add some text to an entry, then select **Share**.

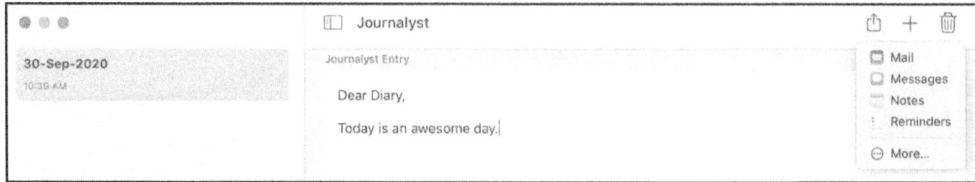

Key points

- Use Mac style toolbars, not iOS navigation bars in macOS apps.

- Toolbars are for the entire window, not just the specific view controller presented to the user.

- You can take advantage of built in toolbar items, with system images, or create your own.

- Users are used to customizing toolbars in many apps. Ensure you provide this capability, as it makes sense.

Where to go from here?

This chapter showed you how quick it is to implement a macOS-centric design in a way that was never so easy. While knowing how to implement your own toolbar items is important, don't forget there are several other system-provided toolbar items provided that you can put to use as well.

You can learn more about these topics from Apple's website at https://developer.apple.com/documentation/appkit/nstoolbaritem/identifier.

Chapter 12: Barista Training: The Touch Bar

By Marin Benčević

You're just one final step away from becoming a true barista master! The one last remaining bar on your journey is… the Touch Bar. Whether or not you love the Touch Bar or think it's a gimmick, many Mac users use it heavily. Because of this, supporting the Touch Bar is an important step in making your Catalyst app feel completely at home on macOS.

In this chapter, you'll expand the app you've been working on to add a few useful items to the Touch Bar. You'll learn about positioning those items and how to allow your users to customize them.

Before you get started, though, let's talk a little about how the Touch Bar works under the hood.

Understanding the Touch Bar

While using your Mac, the Touch Bar is continuously changing depending on what's active on the screen. Similarly to the menu bar, the Touch Bar uses the **responder chain** to determine which items to present. Take a look at Chapter 10, "Barista Training: Menu Bar" to learn more about the responder chain.

The gist is that each view controller and view is a **responder**, and one of them is the **first responder**, which is the currently active view. The responder chain works like a tree, going upwards from the first responder all the way to the root window of your app.

Each item in the responder chain can say "Here are the items I want in the Touch Bar." When the first responder changes, the Touch Bar goes up the chain, picking up items as it goes. Of course, not all of these items fit on the Touch Bar, so the Touch Bar prioritizes items closer to the first responder. The ones at the back don't get shown, and wait patiently for their turn to shine.

However, the ones in the back don't necessarily have to take back stage! If you think an item is more or less important, you can set its priority to a higher or lower value. The Touch Bar will take this into account when ordering the items.

The responders suggest their items to the Touch Bar by overriding makeTouchBar. That method returns an NSTouchBar object. Don't let the naming confuse you: The Touch Bar — the physical bar — displays multiple instances of NSTouchBar. In the following screenshot you'll see four distinct NSTouchBar instances shown on the Touch Bar:

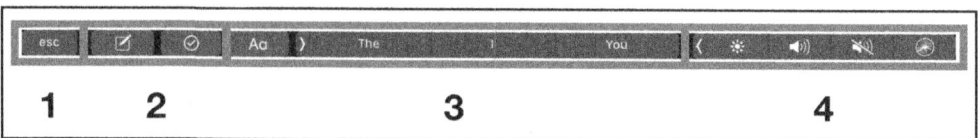

This is the Touch Bar of the Notes app. Bar 1 and 4 are system bars and they're always there. Bar 3 is the bar of an active text field, which is currently the first responder. Bar 3 bullied through and hid some items from Bar 2 because Bar 2 is deeper in the responder chain.

> **Note:** Since the Touch Bar is only available on macOS, NSTouchBar and related APIs are lifted directly from macOS and included in Catalyst, which explains the *NS* prefix. This means that already existing macOS-specific Touch Bar documentation and tutorials are generally applicable to Catalyst apps.

Adding items

Now that we've, ahem, *touched* on some theory, you're ready to add some new items!

Open up the starter project from the provided materials and navigate to **RootSplitViewController.swift**. As mentioned before, each view controller is a responder and, since `RootSplitViewController` is always in the responder chain, it makes sense to add entry-related items there.

You'll start by adding a button that adds a new entry. The first step to adding a Touch Bar item is to define its **identifier**. The Touch Bar uses these identifiers to keep track of which items to show and hide. It also uses the identifier to save customization options for specific items. You'll read more about customization later in this chapter.

Add the following extension at the top of the file, right under the `import`:

```
#if targetEnvironment(macCatalyst)
extension NSTouchBarItem.Identifier {
  static let newEntry =
    NSTouchBarItem.Identifier(
    "com.raywenderlich.Journalyst.addEntry")
}
#endif
```

It's a good practice to extend `NSTouchBarItem.Identifier` instead of peppering a bunch of hard-coded strings around your codebase.

Since the Touch Bar only exists on macOS, you'll wrap most of the code from this chapter in a preprocessor macro that conditionally compiles the code only if it's running on macOS.

Now you can create the item. As mentioned, each subclass of `UIResponder` can override `makeTouchBar` to add items to the Touch Bar.

Next, override `makeTouchBar` in the class like this:

```
#if targetEnvironment(macCatalyst)
override func makeTouchBar() -> NSTouchBar? {
  let bar = NSTouchBar()
  bar.defaultItemIdentifiers = [.newEntry]
  let button = NSButtonTouchBarItem(
    identifier: .newEntry,
    title: "New Entry",
    target: self,
    action: #selector(addEntry))
  bar.templateItems = [button]
  return bar
```

```
    }
#endif
```

Here's what you're doing:

First, you create a new instance of NSTouchBar. The most important property of the bar is defaultItemIdentifiers — an array of all the items' identifiers. If you forget to set this, the items won't show.

Then, you create an NSButtonTouchBarItem object, which is a subclass of NSTouchBarItem. You define the button's title and set its identifier to the one you just created. Just like menu bar items, Touch Bar items use the target-action pattern to determine what happens when tapped. Finally, you add the item to NSTouchBar's templateItems property and return the bar. The templateItems property lets you directly manipulate which items the touch bar will show.

Build and run the app. You should see the item in the Touch Bar.

> **Note**: If you're running on a Mac without a Touch Bar, you can still test this out. In Xcode, choose **Window ▸ Show Touch Bar** and it will show the Touch Bar in a floating window.

Try clicking into the Journalyst Entry text field and note how this causes this item to disappear because it's no longer in the responder chain. When you reactivate any cell in the list of entries, this will cause the "New Entry" item to reappear once again.

You'll notice that you used a subclass of NSTouchBarItem. Generally, you won't use the NSTouchBarItem class directly, since Apple provides a selection of pre-built item types for you. These include:

• NSCandidateListTouchBarItem: Shows a list of options to pick from.

• NSColorPickerTouchBarItem: Lets you pick a color.

• NSSharingServicePickerTouchBarItem: Displays a list of ways to share provided data.

• NSSliderTouchBarItem: Shows a slider between two values.

• NSButtonTouchBarItem: That's the one in the screenshot above. It displays a regular button.

You can also use `NSCustomTouchBarItem` to show a custom view in the Touch Bar item.

Unfortunately, at the time of writing, most of these items are exposed in a limited way in Catalyst, and several of them are completely unusable. Of the above items, the only fully usable ones as I write are `NSButtonTouchBarItem` and `NSColorPickerTouchBarItem`. Hopefully, this will change in future releases.

There are also higher-level subclasses that can contain multiple items. These are `NSGroupTouchBarItem`, which holds a group of items, and `NSPopoverTouchBarItem`, which expands to show more items when tapped. You'll use `NSGroupTouchBarItem` later in the chapter.

Let's get back to what you did in the code. You created your item by adding it to the bar's `templateItems` property. This is the easiest way to create Touch Bar items. But it comes with a drawback. Because the Touch Bar has a direct reference to the item, it stays loaded in memory, even when not shown. That's why you should use `templateItems` *only for lightweight items*.

Implementing the delegate

To avoid this memory issue, you'll implement `NSTouchBarDelegate`. Instead of setting the items directly on the bar, you will only give the bar a list of item identifiers. The bar will then ask the delegate for the item only when it's needed. This is similar to how table views work: Cells are created on-demand instead of being loaded automatically.

First, change the implementation of `makeTouchBar`. Remove the lines where you create and set the button on the bar, and add a new line to set the bar's delegate to `self`. When finished, your method's code should look like this:

```
let bar = NSTouchBar()
bar.delegate = self
bar.defaultItemIdentifiers = [.newEntry]
return bar
```

Next, at the bottom of the file add the following extension to implement the delegate:

```
#if targetEnvironment(macCatalyst)
extension RootSplitViewController: NSTouchBarDelegate {
  func touchBar(
    _ touchBar: NSTouchBar,
    makeItemForIdentifier identifier: NSTouchBarItem.Identifier)
```

```
    -> NSTouchBarItem? {

    switch identifier {
    case .newEntry:
      let button = NSButtonTouchBarItem(
        identifier: identifier,
        title: "New Entry",
        target: self,
        action: #selector(addEntry))
      return button
    default:
      return nil
    }
  }
}
#endif
```

This is similar to `tableView(_:cellForRowAt:)`. The method asks the delegate to create an item based on the provided identifier. In the method, switch on the identifier and, if it matches the one you created earlier, create the item in the same way you did in `makeTouchBar`.

Build and run the app, and you should see the same item you saw earlier.

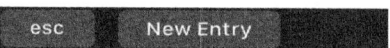

So, you just changed a bunch of your code, and absolutely nothing changed in the bar. Pretty heady stuff, right? :]

Seriously, in spite of a lack of fireworks, the important thing is that your new code is now more memory-efficient. While this might seem like overkill for a single button, in practice you'll typically have a lot more items in your app. Adding items this way from the start will save you from potential headaches down the road.

One more thing: You probably noticed that the Touch Bar automatically positioned your item on the left-hand side. In the next section, you'll see how to position Touch Bar items in a better way.

Grouping items

It's time to add three more items to the Touch Bar: "Delete," "Next Entry" and "Previous Entry." Because all three of these items relate to the currently selected entry, you'll put all of them in a single group item instead of adding them individually.

First, add the following property to the NSTouchBarItem.Identifier extension:

```
static let entryOptions =
  NSTouchBarItem.Identifier(
  "com.raywenderlich.journalyst.entryOptions")
```

You'll use this identifier for the group item. Add it in makeTouchBar by changing the array of item identifiers to this:

```
bar.defaultItemIdentifiers = [.newEntry, .entryOptions]
```

Now that the Touch Bar is instructed to display the item, you can create it in touchBar(_:makeItemForIdentifier:). Start by adding a new case inside the switch statement, right before the default case, and inside this case, create an item for each of the three actions you'll add:

```
case .entryOptions:
  let next = NSButtonTouchBarItem(
    identifier: .init(identifier.rawValue + ".next"),
    title: "Next Entry",
    target: self,
    action: #selector(goToNext))
  let previous = NSButtonTouchBarItem(
    identifier: .init(identifier.rawValue + ".previous"),
    title: "Previous Entry",
    target: self,
    action: #selector(goToPrevious))
  let delete = NSButtonTouchBarItem(
    identifier: .init(identifier.rawValue + ".delete"),
    title: "Delete",
    target: self,
    action: #selector(removeEntry))
```

In this code, you've created these three new items in the same way that you added the "New Entry" button item earlier. Note that the starter project already includes methods for each of these items to call.

Next, you'll create a spacer item and place it between "Previous Item" and "Delete." This is a nice *touch* that helps ensure that your users don't tap on "Delete" accidentally.

To do this, add the following line to the case after the delete item:

```
let spacer = NSTouchBarItem(identifier: .fixedSpaceLarge)
```

Spacer items are built-in Touch Bar items that are created by assigning one of two predefined identifiers to the item: .fixedSpaceSmall or .fixedSpaceLarge.

While all other item identifiers *must be unique*, you can use as many spacer items with the same identifier as you like.

Finally, create a group item and return it by adding the following code to the end of the case:

```
let group = NSGroupTouchBarItem(
  identifier: identifier,
  items: [spacer, next, previous, spacer, delete])
return group
```

Build and run the project, and you should see your new items, including a small space between "Previous" and "Delete."

Since a group contains these items, the Touch Bar treats them all as a single composite item. They will always be shown and positioned together.

While using a MacBook with a Touch Bar, you might have noticed that some items are centered in the Touch Bar. You'll add one final *touch* to your group by centering it.

Each NSTouchBar can define one centered item, and it's called the **principal item**. The good news is that designating an item as principal is very easy. Modify your code now by adding the following line to makeTouchBar, just before its return:

```
bar.principalItemIdentifier = .entryOptions
```

Build and run your project again. You'll now see the group item centered inside the Touch Bar.

By the way, the reason you work with identifiers rather than actual items is that whether items are displayed isn't always up to you. In fact, you can do something here that many developers dread: Give control of this decision directly to your users. In the next section, you'll see how to let users add and remove items from the Touch Bar.

Customizing the Touch Bar

If there's one thing nerds like us enjoy, it's customization options. Apple clearly had this in mind when they created the Touch Bar, as they added app-specific Touch Bar customization. As a developer, it's relatively easy to add support for this.

Apps that support Touch Bar customization have an additional option called **Customize Touch Bar...** inside the **View** menu of the menu bar. To add this option, head over to **AppDelegate.swift** and add the following line at the start of `application(_:didFinishLaunchingWithOptions:)`:

```
#if targetEnvironment(macCatalyst)
NSTouchBar.isAutomaticCustomizeTouchBarMenuItemEnabled = true
#endif
```

Take a moment to savor that supersized property name and read it out loud: "Is automatic customize Touch Bar menu item enabled." It's quite the mouthful, but the benefit of this verbosity is that the property name certainly does explain itself. :]

In spite of its length, enabling this property isn't enough to enable user Touch Bar customization. You'll need to do three more things:

1. Add a customization identifier to the `NSTouchBar` instance.

2. Enable customization for each item you want to be customizable.

3. Add a customization label to each of those items.

Head back to **RootSplitViewController.swift** to do this.

Fist, add an extension at the top of the file, inside the `#if` macro:

```
extension NSTouchBar.CustomizationIdentifier {
  static let journalyst = NSTouchBar.CustomizationIdentifier(
    "com.raywenderlich.journalyst.main")
}
```

Just like the item identifiers, the customization identifier has to be unique for each `NSTouchBar` instance.

Now, set this identifier and make your two items customizable by adding the following two lines to `makeTouchBar`, right before you return the bar:

```
bar.customizationIdentifier = .journalyst
bar.customizationAllowedItemIdentifiers =
[.newEntry, .entryOptions]
```

That takes care of steps 1 and 2.

Next, you'll deal with step 3 by adding a customization identifier to each item you created. In `touchBar(_:makeItemForIdentifier)`, add the following line before `return button`:

```
button.customizationLabel = "Add a new entry"
```

Finally, do the same for the other case by adding this line before `return group`:

```
group.customizationLabel = "Entry Options"
```

These labels show up on the customization screen. If you don't set them, you'll see an ugly warning instead of the labels.

Build and run the project, then select **View ▸ Customize Touch Bar…**

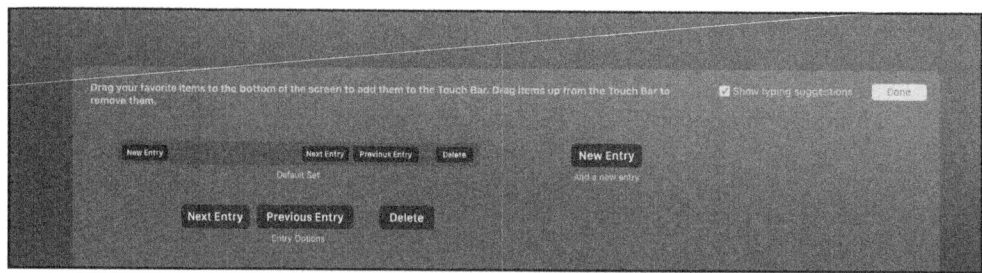

You'll see a screen where you can drag and drop each of your items to and from the Touch Bar. It feels kind of magical to drag an item to something *outside* the screen. Your settings will be saved, so the Touch Bar will stay the same each time you run the app.

> **Note**: If you're using the Touch Bar simulator, you won't drag and drop directly to the floating window. Imagine you have a Touch Bar below your screen — you'll drag to the bottom of the screen as if the Touch Bar was down there.

Congratulations, the Touch Bar was the final bar in your training journey. You're now a certified "bar"ista — feel free to add that to your resume! :]

This also completes Section 2 of this book. By now, your app should look like a native macOS citizen, while also running on iOS devices. How cool is that?

Key points

- The Touch Bar is made of `NSTouchBar` instances.

- The Touch Bar uses the responder chain to determine which items to show.

- Each view and view controller can add items to the Touch Bar by overriding `makeTouchBar` and returning an `NSTouchBar`.

- Use `templateItems` only for lightweight items.

- For other items, implement `NSTouchBarDelegate`.

- Allow customization by enabling the customization menu item, making items customizable, and adding customization labels to the items.

Where to go from here?

To see some other Touch Bar items in action, check out the `NSTouchBar` tutorial written by Andy Pereira, one of the authors of this book: bit.ly/2kxqPjs.

Each Touch Bar item can be further customized by adding images and changing the fonts or colors of the item. You can read about how to do this here: apple.co/2k8Dx8c.

If you consider yourself a pro-level barista, keep in mind that items can be custom views and even include gesture recognizers. Try to think outside the box and make the Touch Bar an essential part of the way users interact with your app.

Section III: Distributing Your App

Congratulations! You now have a Mac app. But getting that app to your users can be a little different than on iOS.

In this section, you'll learn the options for distributing your app and how those options work.

Chapter 13: Releasing on the App Store

If you're reading this book in order, by now you have a pretty good grasp of how to bring an iPhone or an iPad app to macOS. Now it's time for the next step: Getting the app in the hands of users.

The good thing about Catalyst is that once you have a Mac app, it's your choice what to do with it. There are three ways you can distribute your app to your users:

- **The App Store**: The Mac App Store works almost the same way as the one on iOS. All existing iOS apps already follow Apple's app review guidelines, so you should have no issues going through app review. You can either release your app as a standalone Mac App Store product or offer a **universal purchase** so that your customers can buy your app on one Apple platform and have it everywhere else.

- **Third Party Distribution**: As long as you sign the app and get it notarized by Apple, anyone can simply download and launch the app. The distribution, in this case, is up to you.

- **Developer Signing**: Similar to third party distribution, this option requires that you sign your app with a development certificate. The certificate includes a whitelist of specific devices that can install the app, so you can't use this for distributing to the general public. Since macOS doesn't have TestFlight support, this is your best bet for testing the app while it's in development.

Updating existing Catalyst apps

If you made your Catalyst app in Xcode 11.3 or earlier, there are a few steps you need to take to get your app up to speed. Before Xcode 11.4, Catalyst apps had an automatically-assigned bundle ID with a *maccatalyst.* prefix. If you want to offer universal purchase or just want a custom bundle ID, you'll have to make a quick change. Go back to your main target's settings and open the **Build Settings** tab. Scroll down to the **User-Defined** section and set **DERIVE_UIKITFORMAC_PRODUCT_BUNDLE_IDENTIFIER** to **NO**. This will tell Xcode to stop generating a bundle ID automatically, and let you change the bundle ID in the **Signing & Capabilities** tab. From there you can decide how you want to distribute your app.

The App Store vs. third party distribution

Since developer signing is only for testing, you're probably trying to decide whether to use the App Store or distribute the app on your own. There are pros and cons to each approach. The App Store has several benefits including:

- Apple manages the storage and distribution of the app.

- Apple handles payments, including the initial purchase of the app, in-app purchases and subscriptions. They also manage complaints and refunds.

- You can offer a universal purchase and make your app available on both iOS and macOS with a single purchase.

- There's a chance that Apple might feature your app, giving you access to a lot of users that otherwise might not have heard of the app.

- You get access to App Store's analytics and crash reporting with no additional effort.

That said, distributing on the App Store does come with downsides:

- Most notably, Apple takes a cut from all App Store sales (30%), subscriptions (30% then 15% after a year) and in-app purchases of digital goods (30%).

- You're tying the app's destiny to Apple's. If they decide to move the App Store in a different direction, you get no say. Apple could potentially hurt your sales or make your app unavailable.

- It limits your business model options. Offering dynamic or tiered pricing, enterprise deals, or other more creative business models can be difficult or impossible.

While Apple takes a sizable cut of your income, it also gives you the most convenient way to sell your app. It's your choice whether to invest significant effort and be the master of your destiny or save time by letting Apple take care of distribution for you.

If you really can't decide, Apple lets you sell your app on your own *and* on the App Store at the same time.

The chapter you're reading right now will teach you how to distribute your app on the App Store, as well as how to offer a universal purchase. The next chapter deals with distributing your app on your own. If you need help deciding, read both chapters and see how you feel after you know what goes into both approaches.

In other words, now that you've got your app — it's time to make it rain!

Offering a universal purchase on the App Store

By default, Xcode sets up your project to offer a universal purchase, meaning that users buying your app on the iOS app store will get it for free on macOS. With this approach, you might forego the income you'd usually get from a single user, but you give your users a better experience and a better value for the same price. If your macOS and iOS apps are the same and there's a reason to expect users to want to have both versions, consider offering a universal purchase. This section covers the steps you need to take to make your app available in both stores. Later in this chapter, you'll see how to sell your macOS app separately.

The process of distributing your app via the App Store is tedious but simple. All you have to do is click a bunch of things! Before you get started, take note of some basic terminology you'll need when going through this process.

Code signing

Xcode does a good job of automatically **code signing** your app. As the name suggests, code signing is a way of verifying that you've written the code inside the app and it hasn't changed since you wrote it. Code signing is *required* before a user can install an app on a device. Your signature is a **distribution certificate** which you get from Apple and is unique to your developer account.

However, the certificate alone is not enough. You also need an **App ID**: A value that uniquely identifies your app among all other apps on the App Store.

Together, your App ID and distribution certificate make up a **provisioning profile** that you include in the app's binary. The profile verifies that (a) this is your unique app and (b) it was signed by you and didn't change after that signing.

You can see all of these parts in Xcode. Open the starter project (or the app you want to distribute). In the **Project navigator**, click on the name of the project and then on the app target. Open the **Signing & Capabilities** tab.

You can see all the relevant information for signing your app under **Signing**. The **Provisioning Profile** is the same for both iOS and macOS. This makes macOS distribution much simpler.

Setting up an App ID

The first thing you need to do is create an app ID for your app. You can do that in Apple's developer portal. Head over to developer.apple.com, and click on **Account** in the top-right corner. Log in with your Apple Developer ID.

Once you've logged in, navigate to **Certificates, IDs & Profiles** and then to **Identifiers**.

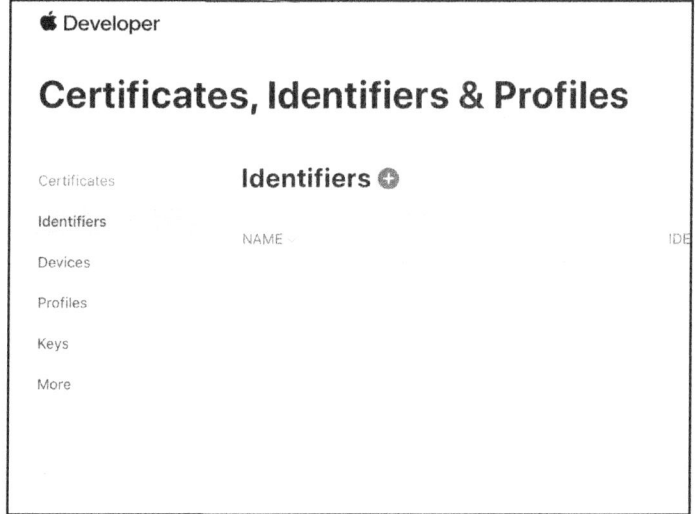

Click the + button next to the header to add a new app ID. Select **App IDs** and click **Continue**.

On the next screen, select **App** as the type. Next, for the **Bundle ID**, enter the one you saw earlier in Xcode. The **Description** isn't public — it's to help you remember which identifier is which — so pick something memorable. Click **Continue**.

> **Note**: If you're using features like CloudKit, push notifications or other capabilities, this screen is where you should enable them. Most of them are self-explanatory and if you don't know what they are, you probably don't need them. You can also enable these later.

The next screen is just an overview of the App ID. If everything looks good, click **Register**. Now, you have a fresh App ID that you can use to create a new app on App Store Connect.

Adding an app entry

> **Note:** If you already have an existing app entry on App Store Connect, skip to the next section.

App Store Connect is where your app's binary meets the App Store. This is where you create new App Store apps, add data like the app title, description or screenshots and — most importantly — upload and release the app.

Head over to appstoreconnect.apple.com and click **My Apps**. Click on the + button in the top-left corner and select **New App**.

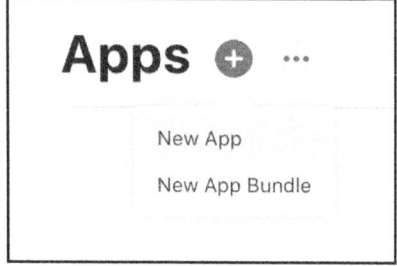

For the **Platforms** select **macOS** and, optionally, iOS. Now comes one of the most important decisions of your app's life: its name. This is the name that will appear on the App Store. Call upon your inner Don Draper and enter something short but catchy. I'll enter **"Journalyst, An app to remember"**. *See what I did there?*

The **Primary Language** determines which language to use to display the app's name and description if there's no localization for the user's locale. For the **Bundle ID**, choose the one you just created in the Developer Portal.

At this point, you might be thinking "What the heck is an **SKU**?" This is short for *Stock Keeping Unit*, and it comes from the retail world, where each product would have a number to identify it. All you need to know is that this should be a value that's unique among your applications. Your bundle ID will do just fine, but feel free to use whatever identifying system you like.

User Access refers to members of your development team. It determines which of your colleagues will be able to edit the app's information. I'll choose **Full Access** because my team of experts consists of only one developer — me. :]

Note: Don't worry about getting something wrong. You can change all of this later, except for the SKU.

Finally, click **Create** to make a new app entry.

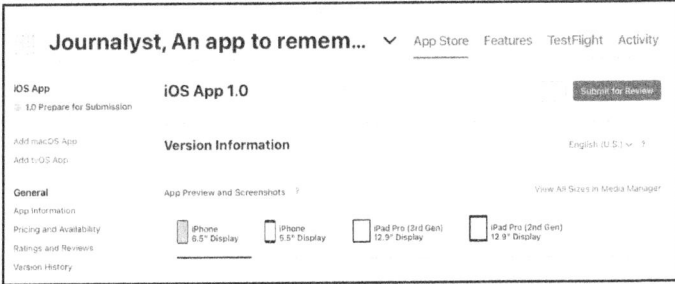

Welcome to your app's dashboard!

There are four tabs at the top of the dashboard:

- **App Store** contains everything related to your app's presentation on the App Store. This includes the app's title and description, keywords, prices and released app versions.

- **Features** is where you can add information related to different app services, like in-app purchases, game center groups, etc.

- **TestFlight** lets you manage beta versions of your app and distribute them to your testers.

- **Activity** shows all of your uploaded builds as well as user ratings.

The next step is to upload your 1.0 build.

Uploading a build

Note: While macOS Big Sur is still in beta, Xcode will not allow you to upload builds to the store. The following instructions are based on previous versions of macOS and may change before Big Sur is released. Once that happens, this section will be updated with the latest information.

Your app entry can hold apps for multiple platforms, as well as versions of each of those apps. To add a macOS app, click **Add macOS App** in the sidebar on the left of your app's dashboard. You'll see a new **macOS App** section and a new version called **1.0 Prepare for Submission**. You now have a place to upload your app.

Next, it's time to go back to **Xcode** to upload a new build of your app to App Store Connect.

First, make sure your project compiles without any errors. Then, in the menu bar go to **Product ▸ Destination** and make sure you've selected **My Mac**. Click **Product ▸ Archive**. This compiles your app and creates an executable that you can upload to the app store. Depending on the size of your app, this process might take a few minutes, so make sure to bring snacks! :]

Once it has finished archiving, Xcode will open the **Organizer** and show your app's archives. Select the one you just created.

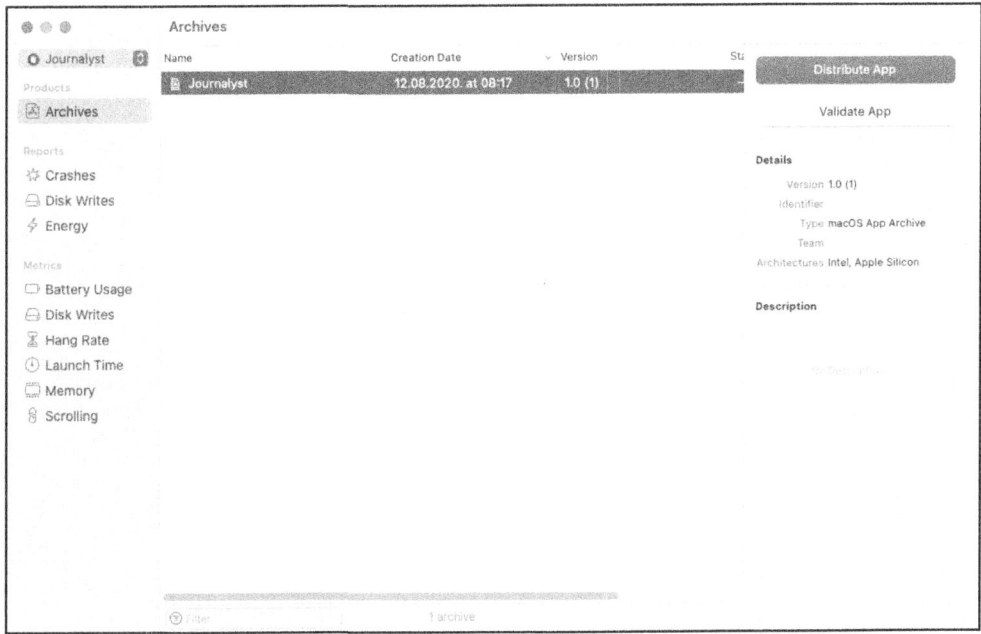

First, click **Validate App**. Make sure you've checked the checkmark for uploading symbols and click **Next**. Select **Automatically manage signing** and click **Next** again. On the next screen, Xcode will ask you to generate a Mac Installer Distribution certificate. Check that checkbox, and click **Next**.

Xcode will create a new Mac Distribution certificate and store it in your Keychain. I recommend you click **Export Signing Certificate...** and save it somewhere secure. This allows you or your colleagues to make builds from other machines, as long as you send them the certificate. Click **Next**. Make sure you've checked **Generate an Apple Distribution certificate** and click **Next** again. Export that one too and — you guessed it — click **Next**.

Finally, you'll see an overview screen of your app's package. Click **Validate** to make sure there are no issues with the app.

Now you're back to where you started, in the organizer window. It's time to upload the app by clicking the big blue **Distribute App** button. Select **App Store Connect** and click **Next**. Select **Upload** and click **Next** again.

I did promise that uploading to the app store is just clicking a bunch of buttons, didn't I?

Make sure you've checked the checkbox for uploading symbols and click **Next**. Select **Automatically manage signing** and on the next screen, click **Upload**. Depending on your connection, this might take a while, so give your clicking finger some rest.

Once it's uploaded, go back to **App Store Connect** and open your newly created app. In the sidebar, click on **1.0 Prepare for Submission** under **macOS App**. This is where you'll edit all the information about the 1.0 version of your app.

There's a bunch of fields to fill out here. Here's some basic information about the most important fields:

- **App Preview and Screenshots**: These are videos and screenshots of your app. For macOS, the screenshots need to be 16:10 and can only be a specific set of predefined resolutions, as described in the **Screenshot specifications** under **Mac** at the following website: apple.co/2KcRFZK. App previews should be 1080p videos with some additional requirements described here: apple.co/2twCcJL.

- **Promotional Text**: This bit of text shows up under the title of your app. It's a short description of what the app does. Aim for something that will make the user click on your app.

- **Description** and **Keywords**: These are very important for **ASO** or *App Store Optimization*. If you describe your app well and choose suitable keywords, it can make your app show up more prominently when users search for related terms.

- **Build**: This is where you select which uploaded binary of your app you're releasing. Click on the + button, select the 1.0 build you uploaded earlier and click **Done**.

- **App Review Information**: This is where you can write notes for the person reviewing your app. I trust you took a good look at the App Store Review Guidelines (apple.co/1lz8Lit). If your app does things that would make a reviewer suspicious, make sure to explain why you're not breaking any guidelines here. Also, if your app has login functionality, create a fake user and provide the username and password. This saves the reviewer time and reduces your chances that they'll reject your app for silly reasons.

The rest of the fields should be self-explanatory. It may seem like a lot of information, but investing time in getting your metadata right could be the difference between a hit and an app nobody ever heard of.

If your app is free, that's all you need to fill out. Feel free to skip the next section. If you have a paid app, take a look at the following section on how to price your app.

Pricing your app

While you're in the **App Store** tab, head over to **Pricing and Availability** in the sidebar. You can set up the price of your app under **Price Schedule**. You can choose from almost 100 different pricing tiers for your app. Each of the tiers has a roughly similar price in all currencies. Once you select a price you can click on **Other Currencies** to see the exact values in each territory.

You can also make your app available for pre-order. This makes your app show up in the App Store even before you release your first version.

If you want to charge a subscription price or offer in-app purchases, you can do that by clicking **Manage** under **In-App Purchases** in the sidebar.

Submitting for review

Once you've filled everything out, click **Save** in the top-right corner and then click **Submit for Review**. A reviewer from Apple will take a look at your app to make sure you're following the guidelines. This can take up to a few days. I know, there's something very frustrating about having a completed app that's just sitting there waiting to be reviewed. Hang in there!

Once your app passes the review, you should get an email notification and the name of the version will change to **1.0 Pending Developer Release**. In the top-right corner, you should see a new button titled **Release This Version**. Click that button and pop a bottle of champagne! You just released an app!

Keep in mind, the App Store might need a few hours to propagate your app, so make sure to wait a while until you start telling all of your friends.

> **Note:** Your app won't be available for universal purchase until you fully release your app on at least two platforms.

Selling your macOS app separately

Instead of offering a universal purchase, you can also sell your macOS app completely separately. You can do this by using a different bundle ID for your macOS app. Head back to **Xcode** and, from the **Project navigator**, click on the name of the project and then on the app target. Open the **Signing & Capabilities** tab. Uncheck the **Use iOS Bundle Identifier** checkbox and enter a new bundle identifier for your macOS app.

> **Note**: You may have to delete the build setting **DERIVE_UIKITFORMAC_PRODUCT_BUNDLE_IDENTIFIER** in order to change the checkbox.

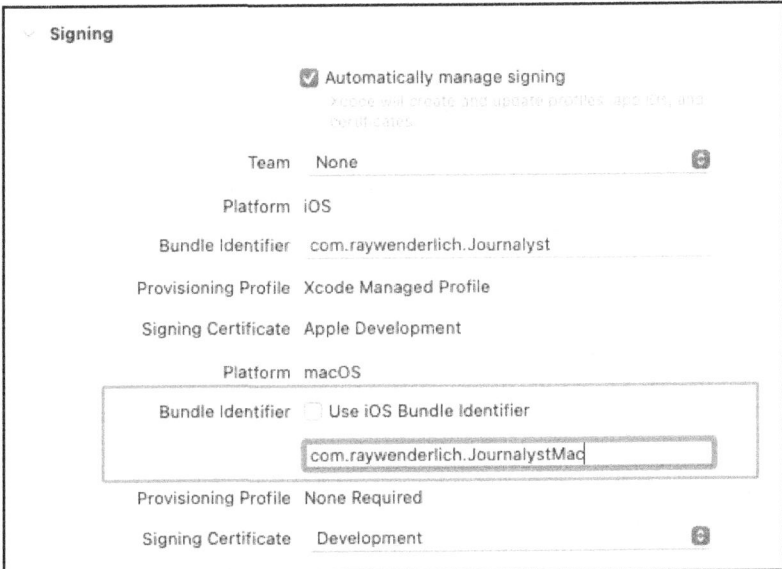

You can distribute your app on the Mac App Store by repeating the steps described in the previous section using this new bundle ID.

Key points

- You must sign each app with a **provisioning profile**, which combines a **certificate** with an **app ID**.

- You create app IDs in Apple's **Developer Portal**.

- Manage the app on the App Store by going to **App Store Connect**.

- Upload **new builds** from Xcode.

Where to go from here?

To make sure you're not violating any of Apple's guidelines, make sure to carefully read through Apple's App Store Review Guidelines: apple.co/1lz8Lit. Apple also provides a helpful list of common app rejection reasons, which you can use as a checklist before submitting: apple.co/2ltWgeB.

Now that you have a grasp on how to upload new builds, think about automating this for **continuous integration** by using tools like Jenkins and Fastlane. You can see an example of how to do this for iOS apps in the Continuous Integration tutorial: bit.ly/2YT52pa.

Since you uploaded your app to the App Store, it's time to think more about optimizing it for App Store's search. Apple provides some useful tips on their site: developer.apple.com/app-store/search/.

Finally, make sure to spread the word about your app anywhere you can! App-making is a tough business, so good luck out there. The whole raywenderlich.com Team is rooting for you! :]

Chapter 14: Third-Party Distribution

By Marin Benčević

If you're reading this chapter, you're probably considering taking destiny into your own hands and releasing your app without the App Store.

It's dangerous to walk that road alone! Take this chapter as a guide. It will talk you through preparing your app so anyone can download it and install it. You'll learn how to notarize your app, how to create a DMG file for your app and also some tips on surviving the harsh world of 3rd party macOS app distribution.

> **Note**: In case you're wondering, push notifications and CloudKit will still work, even if you're not distributing your apps on the App Store.

Before you get started with distributing apps, you'll need an Apple ID enrolled in the Apple Developer Program. Yes, even though you're not using the App Store, you still need a developer account.

The process of distributing apps is complicated by an annoying but useful macOS feature called Gatekeeper. Gatekeeper constantly checks the apps you're running, making sure there's nothing shady inside of them. Have you ever launched an app only to be surprised by an alert telling you the app is from an unidentified developer? That's Gatekeeper.

You've probably noticed not all apps cause this alert to pop up. It usually happens with less-popular or non-native apps. The ones that don't pop up the alert are properly **signed** and **notarized**. In the next section, you'll do that for your app to make sure Gatekeeper lets your users run it.

Signed, notarized and delivered

> **Note**: To learn more about what code signing is and how it works, take a look at Chapter 13, "Releasing on the App Store".

For other people to run your app, you'll need to sign it with a **Developer ID** certificate. That's a special kind of certificate that lets you distribute your app outside the App Store. Only the **Account Holder** of your Apple Developer account can create this certificate.

If you have a *personal* Apple Developer account, you're already the Account Holder. If you're in a team, check your role by going to **App Store Connect**'s **Users and Access** section: apple.co/2Da59iB. If you see yourself in the **Account Holder** tab, you're good.

If you're not the Account Holder, you'll have to ask the Account Holder to export a **macOS Developer ID Application** certificate for you. They can do that from Xcode. Apple provides easy-to-follow instructions on how to export certificates: apple.co/2mj29Mh.

Signing, however, is not enough. You also need to notarize the app. Notarization is a process where you send your app to Apple and let them perform automatic checks on it to make sure it's not doing anything malicious. Once Apple confirms the app is okay, they give your app a ticket. This ticket tells Gatekeeper to relax when a user opens your app, because Apple checked it.

Think of notarization as an airport security check: Your app needs to go through TSA before it can fly across the world to your users' Macs.

In the last chapter, I mentioned code signing guarantees you made your app and *haven't changed it since you signed it*. The latter part is important for notarization: Whenever your app changes, you need to renotarize the app's binary.

Keep in mind that notarization is an automatic process that usually takes a couple of minutes. It's much more relaxed than App Review and you should expect your app to go through notarization without any issues unless you're doing something very suspicious.

Apple made notarization easy; you can do everything in **Xcode**. Open your app in Xcode.

The first thing you need to do is make an archive of your app. Before you do that, make sure your project compiles without any errors. Then, in the menu bar go to **Product ‣ Destination** and make sure you've selected **My Mac**. Click **Product ‣ Archive**. This compiles your app and creates an executable that you can notarize. Depending on the size of your app, this process might take a few minutes — you can think of a cool website domain while you wait. :]

Once it's finished archiving, Xcode will open the **Organizer**. In the sidebar, you should see your app under **macOS Apps**. If you just created an archive, your app should be selected, but you can come back here later and select the app and all your archives will be listed.

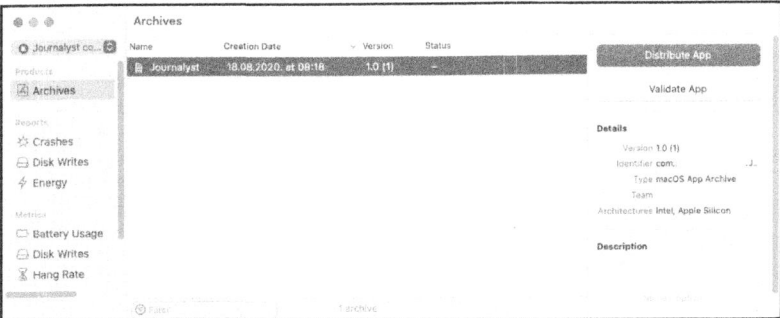

Now that you have an archive, the next steps are signing and notarization. Xcode automatically does this in one fell swoop.

Note: To notarize your app, you need to have **Hardened Runtime** enabled. The Hardened Runtime locks down the app and protects your users from exploits. It's enabled by default for Catalyst apps, so unless you disabled it manually, you should be fine. You can see it in Xcode in the **Signing & Capabilities** tab of your app target's settings.

Click **Distribute App**. In the screen that pops up, select **Developer ID** and click **Next**. Select **Upload** and click **Next**. In the next screen, select **Automatically manage signing**.

> **Note**: At this point, Xcode might show an error saying that you either don't have a Developer ID certificate or you don't have its private key. If that's the case, contact your Account Holder and make sure they export a new Developer ID Application certificate by following Apple's instructions: apple.co/2mj29Mh.

Once signed, you'll get a summary.

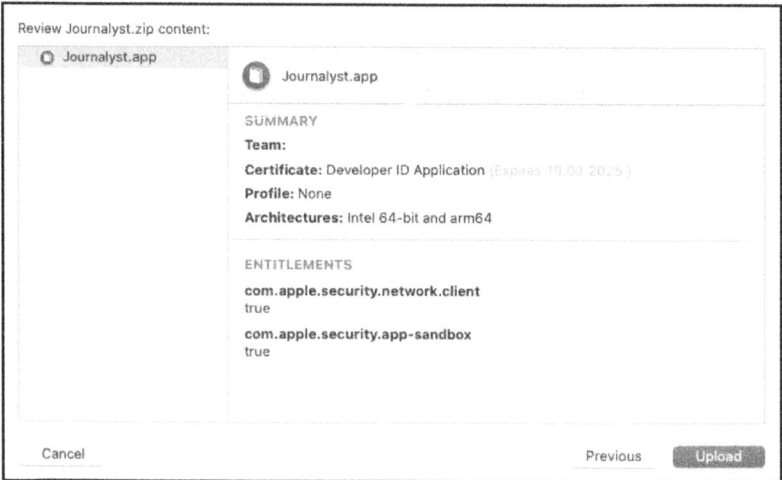

Click **Upload** and Xcode will start uploading the archive to the notary service.

Now you wait. If you've decided on your domain, maybe you can brainstorm some website design ideas at this point. :]

You can check your app's status in the Organizer. If you closed the window, you can open it by selecting **Window ▸ Organizer**. You'll see the status under the **Status** column. You can also click on **Show Status Log** to see what's been going on.

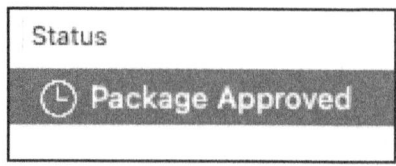

Once notarization completes, it will change to **Ready to distribute**. If something goes wrong, the status will change to **Rejected**. In that case, you can click on **Show Status Log** to see why the notarization service rejected your app.

Now that you have a notarized app, you can export the binary you'll share with your users. Click **Export Notarized App** from the right sidebar. Select a location on disk and you'll have your app!

While you *could* distribute this app as it is, most developers choose to distribute their apps as compressed disk images, aka DMG files. In the next section, you'll see how and why you'd do that.

Creating a DMG file

If you've ever downloaded a macOS app, chances are it came in a .dmg file, which is short for **Disk Image**. When you double-click a .dmg file, it mounts a new disk that contains the app and sometimes additional files like a read-me document.

Packaging your apps in .dmg files has several advantages:

* It lets the user easily install the app by dragging and dropping it to Applications.

* Since apps (.app files) are something between a file and a folder, packing them up into a .dmg makes sure they appear as a single file to web browsers.

* You can password-protect .dmg files.

* .dmg files can contain additional files like read-me documents, licensing information etc.

.dmg files often contain an alias to the user's Applications folder. This lets users easily drag your app right into Applications without having to look for the folder. Apple heavily recommends that you *instruct users to move your app to Applications*. Running the app straight from the DMG might lead to unexpected behavior and could compromise the user's security.

Disk images often include a custom background image to instruct the user to drag and drop the app. In this section, you'll make your very own disk image with an alias to the Applications folder, as well as a custom image.

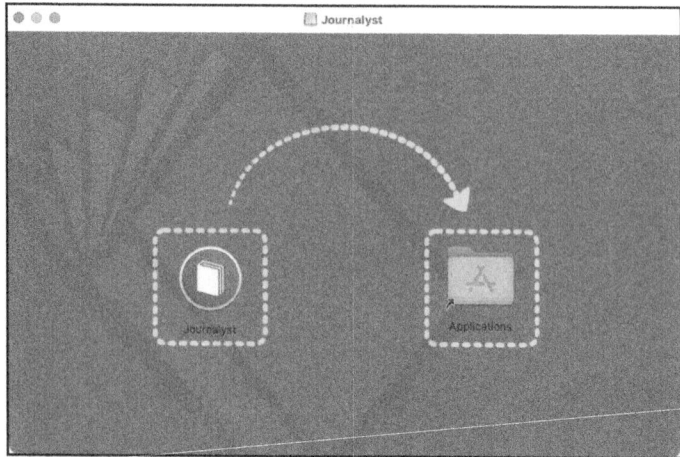

To make a new disk image, open up **Disk Utility**. Click **File ▸ New Image ▸ Blank Image…**. Enter a file name and fill out the **Name** text field. Usually, these two values are the same. Next, for the **Size**, enter a size that is slightly larger than your app. You'll trim the extra size later. You can leave the default values for the other settings and click **Save**.

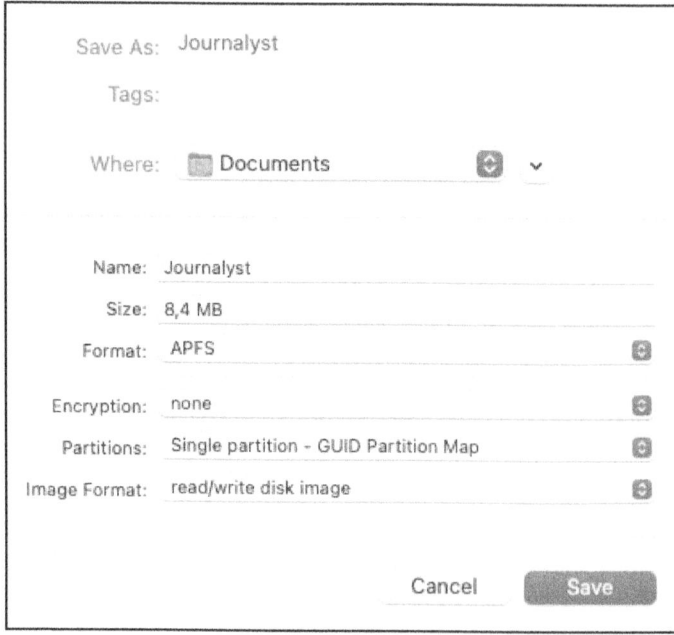

If you go into **Finder**, you'll see that your new disk image has been mounted. Click on your disk image in the sidebar.

Any Finder settings that you change for this disk image will get saved and loaded when users mount your disk image. This includes things like the size of the window, which Finder views and tabs the app shows and other view options. This is all saved on the disk image in a hidden file called **.DS_Store**.

Cleaning up your window

First, let's clean up the window. Press **Command-1** to view the disk image as a grid of icons. Then, in the **View** menu, hide everything that isn't already hidden by clicking **Hide Toolbar**, **Hide Path Bar** and **Hide Status Bar**. You should see a completely blank window.

> **Note**: Depending on your Finder defaults, some of these may already be hidden. Just make sure all the bars are hidden and your window looks like the screenshot.

The next step is to add a custom background image. Press **Command-Shift-.** to show hidden files. Create a new folder in the disk image named **.background**. If a dialog pops up saying the folder will be invisible, click **OK** — an invisible folder is exactly what you need.

If you don't have a background image, you can find one in this chapter's materials. In a new Finder window, navigate to the **starter** folder of this chapter's materials. Copy over **background.png** to the newly-created **.background** folder.

Next, click **View ▸ Show View Options**. Make sure you've checked **Always open in icon view**. Set the **Icon size** to **80×80** and slide the **Grid spacing** slider all the way to the right. For **Background**, select **Picture** and, from a new Finder window, drag over **background.png** from the **.background** folder. While dragging, make sure the disk image is the currently active window.

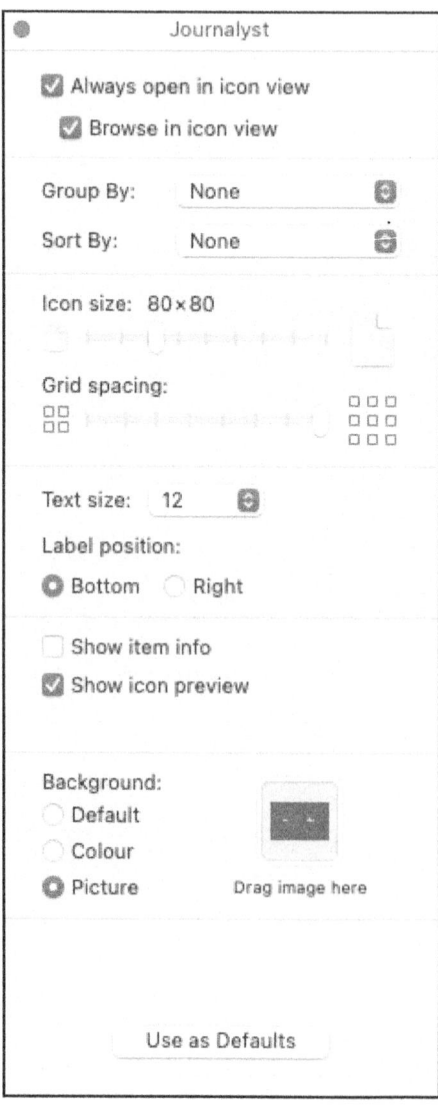

Close the view options window and resize the disk image window so you can't see the edges of the background picture. Press **Command-Shift-.** again to hide the files.

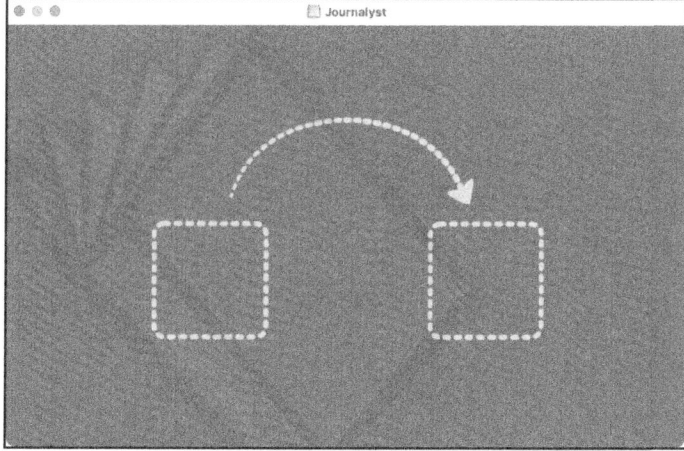

Adding your app

Now that the window looks nice, it's time to add your app and an alias to Applications. From a different Finder window, copy your exported app to the disk image and position it in the left box.

Next, navigate to the root directory of your macOS disk. You can do this from **Terminal** by typing open /. Right-click on **Applications** and click on **Make Alias**. This creates a new folder that acts as a pointer to Applications. Copy the alias to the disk image and position the icon inside the box on the right.

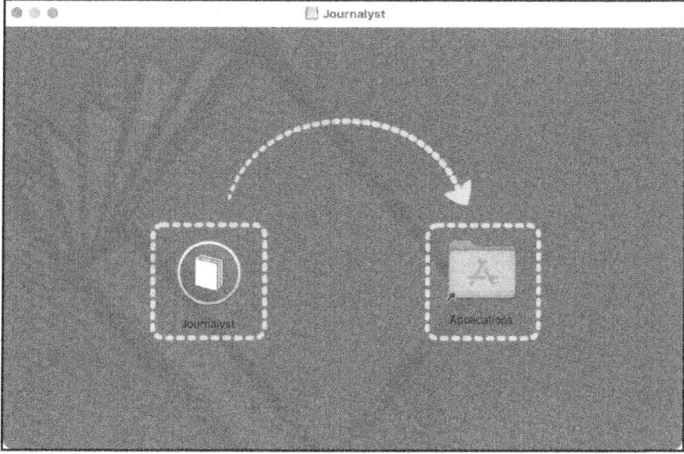

Hey, that's a nice looking .dmg you made! Since you worked hard on setting everything up perfectly, you wouldn't want those pesky users changing things. That's why the next step is to make the image read-only.

Go back into **Disk Utility** and eject your disk image by clicking the little eject button next to the image in the sidebar. Then, in the menu bar, click **Images ▸ Convert…** and select the image you just set up. Name the file anything you like — you can change this later. For the **Image Format**, select **read-only** and click **Convert**. This makes sure nobody can change the image and also trims all the excess space.

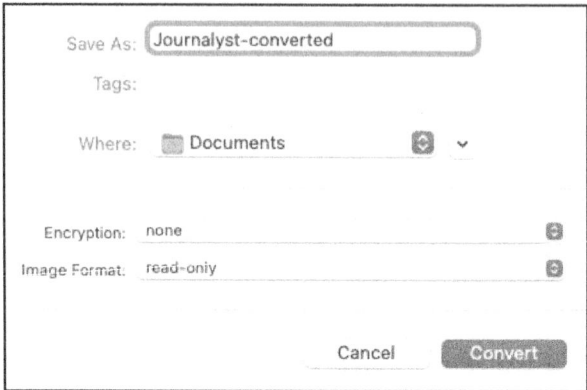

You now have a DMG that you can share with your customers! But unfortunately they won't get far with this DMG. Your users won't be able to run unsigned software. If you're thinking, "I *just* signed my app!" — you're right. But, the .dmg file is *also* a piece of software and needs to be signed and notarized just like your app.

Notarizing disk images

You can sign and notarize a .dmg file pretty quickly, just by using the command line. You'll begin by signing the .dmg file.

Before you start, open **Keychain Access** and, in the top-right corner, search for "developer id". You should see a certificate named "Developer ID Application: Team Name (ID)". Click on the certificate and copy the whole name in bold at the top of the window, including the team ID.

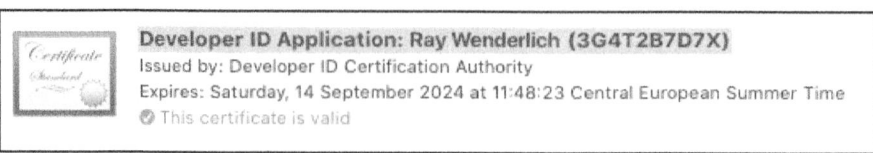

Now, open **Terminal** and use cd to navigate to the folder where you saved your converted disk image. Enter the following command to sign the disk image:

```
codesign \
  -s "Developer ID Application: Ray Wenderlich (3G4T3B2D7X)" \
  Journalyst-converted.dmg
```

Replace the text inside the quotation marks by pasting the name of your certificate; make sure the file name matches your disk image. If everything goes correctly, you won't see any output.

For this next step, you'll need an app-specific password for your Apple ID. Head over to appleid.apple.com and sign in with your Apple ID. Under **Security**, click **Generate password…** under **APP-SPECIFIC PASSWORDS** and name it **altool**. Copy the password to a secure location, you'll need it for the next step.

Now, you can upload the disk image to Apple's notarization service. Instead of using Xcode like before, you'll do it from the command line. Run the following command:

```
xcrun altool --notarize-app \
  -f Journalyst-converted.dmg \
  --primary-bundle-id com.raywenderlich.Journalyst \
  -u ray@raywenderlich.com
```

Pre-empting your commands with xcrun makes sure the commands run from your developer directory. The tool you'll use to notarize your .dmg file is Apple's altool, a command-line tool that lets you interact with the App Store and Apple's notary service.

Replace "Journalyst-converted.dmg" with the name of your disk image, then replace the bundle ID with the one for your app. Finally, unless you're Ray, replace the email with the Apple ID that you use to log into App Store Connect.

You'll see a prompt for a password. Enter the app-specific password you just copied and wait a few moments for the disk image to upload. Once uploaded, you should see a message similar to this one:

```
No errors uploading 'Journalyst-converted.dmg'.
RequestUUID = 66accdd9-7d26-4173-8e88-ea53f61b37b0
```

This confirms that the disk image was uploaded, but it doesn't automatically mean it was notarized. To check the notarization status, run the following command again, replacing the email with your Apple ID:

```
xcrun altool --notarization-history 0 \
  -u ray@raywenderlich.com
```

This shows a table of notarization requests and their statuses. Enter your app-specific password. After waiting for a while and running the command again, you should see the "Status" column change to "success" and "Status Message" change to "Package Approved":

```
Date   RequestUUID Status   Status Code Status Message
-----  ----------- -------  ----------- --------------
(...)  (...)        success 0           Package Approved
```

> **Note**: If notarization failed, you can see more information by entering the following command:
>
> ```
> xcrun altool --notarization-info 66accdd9-7d26-4173-8e88-
> ea53f61b37b0 -u ray@raywenderlich.com
> ```
>
> Replace the email with your Apple ID and the ID with the RequestUUID that was output from the --notarize-app command. You'll see a log file URL that you can open to see a list of issues with your disk image.

A "success" status means that Apple has notarized your disk image and stored a ticket on their servers. You also need to include this ticket in your .dmg file. You can do that by **stapling** it to the file. Run the following command:

```
xcrun stapler staple Journalyst-converted.dmg
```

You should see a message saying, "The staple and validate action worked!". The message makes it sound like Apple itself is surprised the action worked. :]

You now have a signed and notarized disk image that contains a signed and notarized app. It's like a babushka doll of security!

Key points

- To distribute macOS apps without the App Store, you need to sign the app with a **Developer ID** certificate.

- Apps and other software packages need to be **notarized** to verify they're malware-free.

- You can use Xcode to notarize apps.

- You package apps inside disk images (.dmg files) for easier downloading and installation.

- Sign .dmg files using the `codesign` command-line tool.

- Notarize .dmg files using the `altool` command-line tool.

- After notarization, make sure to staple the ticket to the .dmg file by using the `stapler` utility.

Where to go from here?

Unfortunately, unless you want to distribute your app via email, you'll also need a website to host and show off your app. If you're making a paid app, you'll need to deal with payments and managing licenses. This sounds scary, but there are some tools to help you.

Here are a few tools you can use to manage customers and billing:

- Paddle (paddle.com/solutions/mac/) lets you manage billing customers both in-app and on your website.

- Even though it's not specific to macOS apps, Gumroad (gumroad.com) lets you easily sell stuff online and manage your customers.

- Braintree (braintreepayments.com) is a company owned by PayPal and also offers an easy way to set up payments.

All of these have ways to integrate them into existing websites and, in some cases, macOS apps.

If you're not a web developer, don't fret. There are plenty of tutorials, courses and website builders to get you started. First of all, you already know Swift, so why not use it to build your website? Vapor, a server-side Swift framework, offers a templating engine called Leaf that you can use to build a landing page for your app. Here are three different resources on Vapor and Leaf:

- Templating Vapor Applications with Leaf tutorial: bit.ly/2kKUfL2.

- Server Side Swift with Vapor video course: bit.ly/2kdhaOK.

- Server Side Swift with Vapor book: bit.ly/2FI9wAR.

If you're not into the idea of building out a website with code, you can use website builders like Squarespace (www.squarespace.com) or Webflow (webflow.com). Aside from letting you build a website without knowing anything about web development, these tools also host your website — one less headache to worry about.

As you can see, exporting your app is not enough. You also need to deal with building websites, managing customers and marketing your app. Nobody ever said it would be easy, but indie app development is extremely rewarding. Your success is in your own hands, for better or for worse. We at raywenderlich.com are all rooting for you. Good luck out there! :]

Conclusion

You made it! Congratulations on finishing the book. We hope you've enjoyed your journey from iPhone to iPad to Mac - to a whole new field of users!

In this book, you learned how to take an iPhone app and add the features that make it work great on both iPad and Mac. That's the great thing about Catalyst - most of your efforts will be useful on multiple platforms now!

You also learned about those things that are specific to the Mac platform, and how to take advantage of them in your app.

In the end, you have one codebase that works great on iPhone, iPad and Mac! That's living the dream, baby!!

Now, you're ready to go out on your own - take your iOS apps to the Mac, and make them insanely great!

If you have any questions or comments about the projects in this book, please stop by our forums at http://forums.raywenderlich.com.

Thank you again for purchasing this book. Your continued support is what makes the books, tutorials, videos and other things we do at raywenderlich.com possible. We truly appreciate it!

— Nick, Marin, Andy, Brian, Ehab and Jerry

The *Catalyst by Tutorials* team

Printed in Great Britain
by Amazon